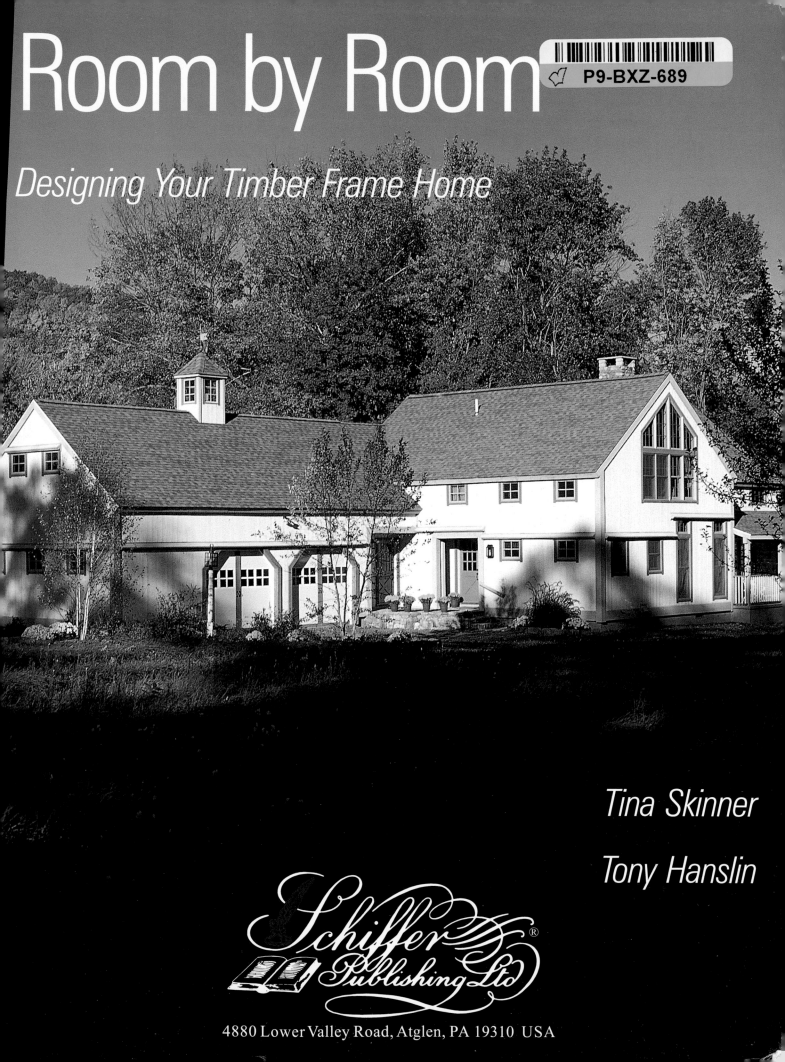

Room by Room

Designing Your Timber Frame Home

Tina Skinner

Tony Hanslin

Schiffer Publishing Ltd

4880 Lower Valley Road, Atglen, PA 19310 USA

©Suki Coughlin/ Paula McFarland Stylist

Library of Congress Cataloging-in-Publication Data

Skinner, Tina.
  Room by room: designing your timber frame home / by Tina
Skinner and Tony Hanslin.
     p. cm.
  ISBN 0-7643-2006-8
1. Wooden-frame houses—Design and construction. 2. Large
type books. I. Hanslin, Tony. II. Title
TH4818.W6 S58 2004
728'.37—dc22

                                    2003025864

Designed by Tina Skinner and Mark David Bowyer
Type set in Zurich LtCn BT/Zurich BT

ISBN: 0-7643-2006-8
Printed in China

Published by Schiffer Publishing Ltd.
4880 Lower Valley Road
Atglen, PA 19310
Phone: (610) 593-1777; Fax: (610) 593-2002
E-mail: Info@schifferbooks.com

For a large selection of fine design books on this and related
subjects, please visit our web site at **www.schifferbooks.com**
We are always looking for people to write books on new and
related subjects. If you have an idea for a book please contact us
at the above address.

This book may be purchased from the publisher.
Include $3.95 for shipping.
Please try your bookstore first.
You may write for a free catalog.

In Europe, Schiffer books are distributed by
Bushwood Books
6 Marksbury Ave.
Kew Gardens
Surrey TW9 4JF England
Phone: 44 (0) 20 8392-8585; Fax: 44 (0) 20 8392-9876
E-mail: info@bushwoodbooks.co.uk
Free postage in the U.K., Europe; air mail at cost.

Welcome

The factory where Yankee Barn Homes are born. ©Yankee Barn Homes

Dear Reader,

Thank you for your interest in *Room by Room: Designing Your Barn Style Home*. Since 1969, Yankee Barn Homes has been working with homeowners across the country to create their ideal country homes. We have put our more than thirty years of experience in design and engineering into this book, which we hope will help you create the home of your dreams.

In 1969, when my father Emil Hanslin began Yankee Barn Homes, he dreamt of barn architecture serving as the basis for beautiful and durable homes. Today we are realizing that dream from coast to coast and across the seas. Over one thousand Yankee Barns stand, each a unique vision of the homeowner as we continue in the combination of tradition and innovation -- the hallmarks of Yankee Barn Homes.

Tony Hanslin
CEO, Yankee Barn Homes

©Yankee Barn Homes

A house is delivered almost complete. On site, the frame is erected, and then roof and wall panels applied. In this case, siding was not included as the homeowners chose a custom finish for the exterior.

Acknowledgments

Editorial Team: Tony Hanslin
                         Tina Skinner
                         Lindy McCord
                         Melissa Cardona

Technical Advisors: Rob Knight
                         Russ Prudhomme

Architectural Consultant: Rob Reno, AIA

Photo Editors: Amanda Gillen
                         Tina Skinner

©Yankee Barn Homes

Rule #1: Work in pencil.

You are going to come back dozens of times and rethink rooms. Even the most experienced designer or architect is going to have to rethink the details when squeezing all those dreamed-of rooms within the allotted space, and then creating a balanced outward display of windows and doors. Other supplies might include tracing paper, a small ruler for creating straight lines, a hot cup of cocoa, or a nice glass of Merlot.

Rule #2: TWO!

Remember there are two people, maybe more, who need to be happy with the finished home. Everyone should get their say, and everyone should have some satisfaction in seeing their ideas and dreams realized. And on that note, everyone has to do a little compromising! Be gentle with each other.

Rule #3: Don't Get Frustrated.

Okay, don't *stay* frustrated. Work on this book when you're in the mood, together, then put it away and think about it when you're not. It might be hard to find the best time, or place, to do this. So keep the book handy. When you're together in the kitchen, grab the book and think about your dream kitchen. When you're in the dining room, think about how you might plan a better dining room. Imagine how you'd incorporate your living room furniture into a future abode (or trash it and get what you've always wanted!).

Rule #4: Be Firm, but Flexible.

You're planning your dream home. Be firm and go for the things you've always wanted in a home. For those things that don't matter as much, be flexible. This will help your designer or architect work with you to make sure you're getting the home of your dreams, within a budget that makes it possible to break ground.

Rule #5: Have Fun.

After all, isn't that why you're doing this in the first place? If you wanted easy, you'd buy what's being built cookie-cutter style right down the street. This home should be all about you and your family.

Table of Contents

How You Live

It is assumed that, by choosing this book, you are expressing an interest in a timber frame home. You are excited by the possibility of expansive interior volumes, cathedral ceilings that may extend as high as twenty-nine feet, and great walls of glass that connect your vision for the interior with a love of the outdoors.

By setting out to design and build your own house, you are obviously seeking the unique. Anyone can walk into a development, chose a few alternatives to a standard model, and wait for the builder to finish his work. You're electing to invest more of yourself, and your time, into making sure your home reflects who you are and how you live. You will hand select your plot of land and set out to build a one-of-a-kind home. In taking this time, you also expect your home to be structurally and aesthetically superior. Most importantly, it will be precisely perfect for your needs.

You will want to choose design professionals you trust and feel comfortable working with. You want to sign on with architects, interior designers, and/or landscapers who will take the time to get to know your family. You'll be asking yourself questions about who will live there, and who is likely to occupy the house in the near and distant future. If you're young and just getting started, maybe you need a smaller home with plans for future additions as your family multiplies. Perhaps your children are nearly grown, in which case their rooms will become available for alternative uses. Or maybe an aging parent, or your own advancing years, require ground-level accommodations that offer universal or wheelchair access.

Do you entertain often? If you entertain for business, perhaps it is important to impress your guests, and to tuck private family areas well away from the more "public" areas of your home. Or are your guests friends and family who travel far to visit, and need sleepover accommodations. Perhaps a private suite, or separate quarters over the garage would be in order?

Perhaps this is a second home, a vacation retreat, and one that you hope to retire to later. All of these lifestyle factors play major roles in shaping the home of your dreams.

The following survey was designed to help you envision your future home. Richly illustrated, it offers an opportunity for you and family members to sit down and evaluate architectural aspects drawn from hundreds of homes and to assess your individual tastes and needs.

As you assess these, you will want to rank your needs in order of preference. Whether building a million dollar home, or one worth merely a quarter of that, every home builder finds they have to tap the breaks during the planning stage. As you work your way through the questionnaires, use a rating system that you all can agree on, so later when it comes to trimming, or adding, you can turn to the Cs and As among your choices. You may want to give up that dormer in order to have the high-end kitchen appliances, a wing of the house in order to have that two-story stone fireplace and chimney.

Armed with this, you are prepared to approach your design professional and to begin pinning down the details that will suit both your lifestyle and your budget — two factors that may be at odds with one another!

Dream House (A Game)

The following is just a fun test, a game. To fully enjoy it, make sure you take it together. Ask each question, then share your answers. There are no correct answers, so use your imagination. And make sure you don't read the answers until you're finished!

1. Envision yourself walking through the woods for these first two questions. Now, as you stroll along, you encounter an animal. What is it?

2. Now you encounter a second animal What is it?

3. As you continue down the forested path, you find something blocking your path. What is it?

4. How do you negotiate the obstacle?

5. The path now leads to your home. You are approaching the front door. Describe this door's appearance. Is it open or closed, locked or unlocked?

6. Now, upon entering the house you are greeted by a vase of flowers. What kind of vase is it? Big or small? What is it made of?

7. How many flowers are in the vase?

8. Pass through the house to the backyard, where you have a lovely little body of water. There are ducks on the pond – how many?

1. The first animal you envision symbolizes you.
2. The second animal you encounter symbolizes your partner.
3. The obstacle on your path is symbolic of your roadblocks in life. What have you created for yourself?
4. This says a lot about how you will approach those little, and big, problems that inevitably crop up in the process of custom-building a home.
5. The door symbolizes your feelings, i.e., your heart. Did you choose a hard, steely substance, or a soft wood? Does your door have windows, or present a solid face? Is it locked, ajar?
6. The vase represents your wealth. If you chose a vase of pottery, you've selected a rather humble budget, a golden vase would make you an emperor.
7. The number of flowers represents the number of friends or lovers in your life.
8. The number of ducks is the number of children you will or do have.

Maybe you're scoffing that this was a whole lot of hooey, but I'd wager that you had fun. Further, I assure you that, having played this game with hundreds of people over the last ten years, in every case there was more truth than fantasy in the answers. The moral of this test as it applies to your current, custom-homebuilding undertaking is, "To thine own self be true." Moral number two: remember to have fun. And number three: it's your dream, make your vase out of diamonds if you want. Blow up that concrete barrier with fifty tons of dynamite!

About Timber Framing

Timber framing is an architectural style dating back over 2,000 years. Mortise and tenon joinery techniques for roof systems were familiar to ancient Egyptians and Romans, and the technique was used in early Japanese temples as well as English manor homes. In the 10th century, a self-supporting post and beam structure was developed that proved advantageous in its independence from sunken ground poles (which rot). It also required less wood than log structures, a commodity that was becoming increasingly rare for Europeans. A seemingly limitless supply of wood in the new world, and improved construction techniques made timber framing a standard on the early American landscape. Energy saving innovations have made it even more accessible as well as practical for today's homeowners.

By purchasing this book, you've already expressed a preference for a timber frame home. Are you a purist, set on having your home rest in the strong arms of post and beam timbers, or are you willing to cover up standard framing and provide decorative beams for effect? Certainly you can save money by choosing partial post and beam, yet provide the same feel for rooms in the house where you will spend most of your time.

The placement of the timber frame is fundamental to load bearing and aesthetics, and is a factor in costs. Your designer will help balance your aesthetic and budgetary needs with a design that incorporates as much timber frame as possible.

A full post and beam frame extends the full width, length, and height of the structure. Because most of the weight of the structure rests on the post and beam frame, you can eliminate some inside walls to help support the roof and, if you like, leave the entire interior open. Timberwrights are fond of their trade, and styles vary dramatically. In many cases, the primary focus of the home is on decorative post and beam details. In the case of Yankee Barn homes, the timber frame is more minimalist — a style popular with many wives as it leaves more room for interior décor. In "barn style," Yankee Barn Homes incorporates traditional sidings and architectural elements such as transom windows and pentroofs that trace their roots to barn architecture. The style strikes a chord in the heart of many people seeking a "country style" home.

In a classic A-frame, salt box, or cape style home, posts and beams are organized perpendicular to the ridge at equal distances. This style provides less flexibility for placing windows, but more floor space. To create more window opportunities, other style frames can be used, punctuated by decorative or non-structural beams. Many people choose to do a central great room in their home with post and beam construction, and the rest of their home in stick style with decorative beams to extend the aesthetic throughout. These walls and beams can be cut and assembled on site, or panelized in a factory and delivered for assembly. Panelized walls with no timber frame may be used for outlying rooms or structures, such as a garage or horse barn.

The following will help set your goals in determining what is best for your home. This book will also help you to analyze what you most want, room by room, with respect to where you want to see your posts and beams exposed.

__   Want full post and beam frame
__   Partial frame is acceptable
__   Exposed beams for the great room
__   Decorative beams to be incorporated in select rooms

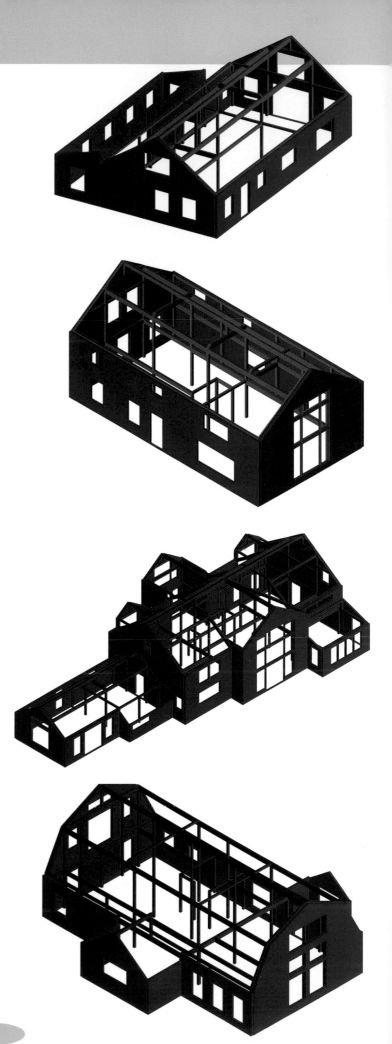

©Suki Coughlin/ Paula McFarland Stylist

A-frame trusses were left exposed in this pool room.

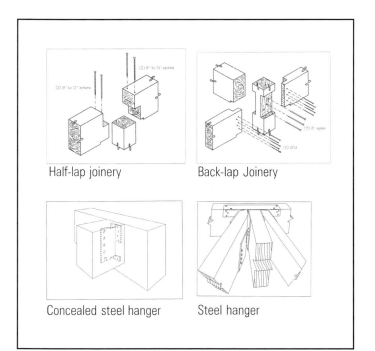

Half-lap joinery

Back-lap Joinery

Concealed steel hanger

Steel hanger

Finishing nails virtually disappear in a beam, whereas the rugged look of wrought iron lends an authentic feel.

Selecting your timbers

Many people prefer a substantial use of reclaimed timbers. These timbers bear the marks of time, adding instant character and weathered charm. Reclaimed timbers have the added advantage of years of aging, providing a strong, seasoned lumber and avoiding the effects of drying such as checking and twisting. The antique lumber has holes and gouges from prior use in old buildings. The reclaimed wood is not graded and may include various species.

For those who want a fresh and perfect finish, new beams have appeal. These can be found in a variety of woods that are kiln dried to lower the moisture content and minimize checking, twisting, and warping.

Laminated beams are manufactured from new lumber using a number of smaller boards glued under pressure and planed to create one very strong timber.

The texture of your frame is important to the overall look and feel you want to establish. There are various beam finishes to choose from. The illustrations help, but you may want to visit a few timber frame homes to really get the sense of how these beams fit into the overall room. Check the beam finish that appeals to you:

__ Rough sawn has a more rustic look, preserving the rough texture left by the mill's saw blade.

__ Skip-planed is also rustic in appearance, but the timbers are lightly planed, leaving some saw marks and roughness.

__ Beams and posts can also be planed smooth and chamfered, where the corners are slightly rounded or beveled for a more formal appearance.

Timbers can be stained any number of wood tones, or in color for that matter, though most people choose from a warm, medium-toned palette. Look at the various examples of interior images on this page and throughout the book to evaluate which tones appeal most to you. Which would look best with your style of furnishings? It is possible to use different finishes in different rooms of your home, too. As you proceed through the book, you will have an opportunity to express finish preferences for your exposed beams.

Nails and Fasteners

In the pure world of timber framing, there are no metal fasteners used. Posts and beams are mortise and tenon-cut to fit perfectly, and are secured by wooden pegs or dowels. This is a costly, time-consuming method of construction. Yankee Barn uses lap or half-lap joinery, with concealed mechanical fasteners for strength. This kind of pre-construction is more quickly assembled.

In many contemporary constructions, or for places in the frame with exceptionally long spans or unusually heavy loads, heavy duty steel plates and nails may be used to ensure the frame's stability. Though most fasteners are concealed, there will be some places where these fasteners are exposed in the interior of the house. You may prefer that the nails in your timber frame have inconspicuous heads. These work well with smooth-planed frames. For a more traditional, rugged look, you might choose wrought iron nails with decorative black heads, a perfect complement to rough sawn frames.

Steel hangers and concealed fasteners add strength to a beam connection with unusually heavy loads, or no post below. Hangers are usually painted black with square-headed black lags or bolts, but can be done in any color.

Stone facing and a center door provide a façade of classic colonial design. Behind the simplistic front, a sprawl of ells and wings adds space and contemporary comforts.

A cupola crowns a horse barn containing garage and workshop space. The Entryway to the home sits in the sheltered lee of two wings. A massive, second-story picture window commands a view of the approach, while protecting its owners from casual peeping.

The second story overhangs the first, with a second floor balcony emphasizing the importance of the view. From the front, you would think the home was a ranch, but the slope in back allows the building to open up to a waterfront view.

How do you imagine your house looking as you approach it? You probably won't have the opportunity to create the road that leads to your house, but you can start at the beginning of your driveway. From that point out, you are creating your world.

Your Lot

If you haven't yet chosen your piece of land, you can still work on your dream home. However, you may need to make adjustments when the land is acquired. Your site will influence where rooms are located to take advantage of views, sunlight, road access, and perhaps to maximize privacy. A sloping lot may create an opportunity for a walkout basement.

Together with your architect or designer, you will work to capitalize on the best your lot has to offer in terms of passive energy savings, view advantages, and privacy. You may also need to overcome obstacles such as a steep grade that requires retaining wall structures or support columns. If your lot is wooded, and you want it to stay that way, careful planning may be required to ensure that as many trees as possible are preserved. Likewise, the planning stages are the best time to consult with a landscaper regarding your future lawn and garden space — you might as well sculpt the grounds to suit your future needs while you have the equipment on hand to create septic fields, wells, and your new driveway and foundation.

If your site is ready to be developed (cleared of trees), take pictures and attach them here. Label them to show which views you want to see from which rooms.

The following questions will help design professionals understand your lot:

__   Level
__   Sloped
__   Wooded
__   Open Field
__   Near/On a body of water
__   In mountains
__   Special views
__   Rural or country neighborhood
__   Suburban neighborhood
__   Urban site
__   Don't know yet

©Suki Coughlin/ Paula McFarland Stylist

The classic Colonial offers a public visage of symmetry and solidity. The classic red door zeros in on the entrance, approached stage-like by an entry patio and circular brick stairs.

©Suki Coughlin/ Paula McFarland Stylist

The driveway passes right by the front door and delivers occupants to the family entrance of this cape style home through the garage. Guests stop short, where a walkway makes an obvious distinction regarding their welcome approach.

Your Driveway

Your driveway is generally roughed in before construction to allow builders access. After work is pretty much finalized on the structure, the driveway is finished. Together with the house itself, a driveway helps to form your first impression of a home. The following are some choices you will make when planning the driveway:

__ Straight from road to garage, the most efficient and cost saving route.

__ Curvy and pretty, set aside to preserve the look and landscaping, the curb appeal of the home, and a bit more costly with the added square feet.

__ Gravel

__ Asphalt

__ Concrete

__ Paver or other decorative material

Siting the House

Rate the following from 1-10, 10 being qualities that are most important to you.

__ Siting of the house should maximize the use of passive solar energy.

__ Siting of the house should take maximum advantage of existing vistas.

__ We want our home to be concealed from the road and/or neighbors.

__ We want to maintain the natural integrity of our plot (keep trees and shrubs as intact as possible).

__ Our lot will require considerable landscaping.

__ Deed restrictions and local ordinances play a major role in dictating the house siting.

__ Difficult terrain conditions will dictate house siting.

__ Our home will be visible from the road.

__ Our home will be hidden from view.

__ Our home will look as though it has been on the landscape for generations.

__ Our home will create impressive visual impact.

__ Our home will blend in with Nature.

Courtesy of House Beautiful's Building Manual; ©1985 by the Hearst Corp.

A barn-like exterior, with gambrel roof, reveals its residential nature with a bump out front entryway. Stone finish adds a sense of history to the structure.

©2003 F&E Schmidt

A prow-front bump-out great room in the center of this home gives an awesome first impression. Garage doors face parallel to the street, allowing the parking space to become more decorative and consistent with the exterior of the home.

©Suki Coughlin/ Paula McFarland Stylist

Set back in the woods, this home merges the definition between front and back. Instead of a porch, a deck wraps the front of the home. The front door is actually discovered upon rounding the bend of driveway. The first impression is of the stone fireplace, a symbol of warmth within, and a two-story round-top window, promising a luxury of light and space. Two gable ends in front, and the eave end of the barn in the rear add variety to the profile.

©Brad Simmons

Banks of wood and windows crown a hilltop, offering an impressive overlook of the road below.

The following questions will help you distill your vision for your dream home:

We envision our home having ___(#) stories.

Architectural elements we would like to include:
__ A gabled roof
__ Dormer windows
__ Wood siding
__ Stone
__ Brick
__ Entry portico
__ Custom front door
__ Standard doors to save money
__ Front porch
__ Extended eaves for shading

From the Front

The following homes are examples of front profiles that may or may not match your vision for a home. Terminology in the captions will help you express features you like about the homes, helping you and your designer create a home that expresses your tastes. Please make notes near the images you like, and try to explain why. Circle features of the home that are appealing to you, and ask your architect to incorporate them into your home design.

©Suki Coughlin/ Paula McFarland Stylist

A symmetrical, lakefront home needed to expand, so the owners chose an adjoining, barn-style addition. Together, the married structures create the feeling of history. The original structure was wrapped in shingles, the "barn" addition in shiplap siding.

©Yankee Barn Homes Photo by Ross Chapple

Designed to crown a hilltop, this three-level home is clearly in command of all approaches. Only intended visitors will approach, and their pathway is clearly defined by a long stretch of driveway. The house itself suggests the luxury of sprawl, crowned by a "sugar house loft," a modern-day widow's walk that offers 360-degree views and filters light into the second floor rooms.

A straight shot to the garage puts these homeowners inside. From there, the family home feels private, with few windows or access points to the road beyond. Two pentroofs are prominent upon approach. Originally used in barn architecture, these slanted pieces of trim would protect the metal rollers and grooves above sliding doors. Today they protect the windows.

These homeowners have adorned their home with country touches, from a twig-built garden fence to a rock-lined gravel driveway. The windows attest to their love of the countryside.

Stone is paired with wood in a new addition to a historic home. Clapboard siding and traditional styling make the addition appear a generation old.

From the Back Side

The front of the home is all about curb appeal and appearances. The back of the home is where we spend the majority of our outdoors time. Family rooms, kitchens, and bedrooms usually open out to the rear of the home, as does the occasional master bedroom. This is where we put our barbecue and horseshoe pits, our comfy lawn furniture, and our family memories.

A bleached finish allows shingle siding to stand out in this wooded setting, and cornice returns add a touch of extra architectural detailing to the roofline.

A deck spills off the back of the home, where French doors flank a massive stone fireplace and afford speedy access to the outdoors.

Decking skirts the entire home, placing the emphasis on being outside. A 19 by 9 foot roundtop window connects inside with out. A greenhouse was attached to the side to create year-round warmth and foliage.

A winged porch is protected by a hip roof that shelters a big back patio, and provides an attractive, flared skirt to the rising structure behind it. This home, like so many, was designed to fit the character of its neighborhood and yet house the unique features sought by the homeowners.

By extending the roof, a long stretch of standing seam metal roof protects the main structure as well as a sunroom. Shiplap siding emphasizes the vertical rise of the great room, as well as the garage and guest suite beyond.

Built into a slope, a deck allows the occupants to walk out their first floor onto an elevated deck.

A prow moves your eye from the gently sloped roof to the exciting glass-gabled wall. A central chimney marks the location of a great fireplace below.

Rising among dunes, this shingle home is dominated by glass, offering occupants the salty air and fantastic seaside views they sought when they designed. A dormer deck combination provides a great place for coffee off the master bedroom.

The siding and trim afford protection against the weather and also present a significant aesthetic choice. Vertical sidings tend to be rustic and barn-like. Horizontal clapboards look more formal. Shingles fall between vertical siding and clapboards in formality, and are often a choice at the seashore. Sometimes a particular look can be achieved by mixing different types of siding on different parts of the building.

Wood finishes

Cedar is a popular choice for exterior wood finishes because it is durable and pest resistant. Pine is used on many classic New England barns.

Shiplap or vertical siding is the least expensive option when working with Yankee Barn Homes, and is very popular because it creates the authentic barn look. It is pre-installed at the YBH shop, saving on labor costs.

Horizontal siding must be installed on site by the builder after the barn raising. Horizontal wood treatments include clapboard and shingles. Clapboard is frequently painted, though it can be stained. White Cedar Shingles are long lasting, and provide the popular Cape Cod look. They can be dipped in stain, so that they are coated on all four sides, or a bleaching agent can be applied to keep the color uniform.

Other siding options include stucco, stone, cement fiber board in claps or shingles, brick, aluminum, vinyl, or a combination of the above. If you will be using a stone or stucco siding, or other siding supplied by your builder, then all you need from Yankee Barn is the plywood exterior.

__   Shiplap (vertical) siding
__   Clapboard
__   Shingle
__   Other

Trim

Trim is used where the roof and the top of the wall meet, around windows, at corners, and on all four sides of the house. Two styles of trim are popular: a more formal style called traditional, and the attractive barn-style trim. This simple style utilizes heavy 2" trim. It is usually used with vertical siding, but can be used with shingles for a more rustic look. The 5/4" trim is usually used with clapboards or shingles, and does not include pentroofs or skirtboards. Skirtboards are horizontal trim used at the foundation level with shiplap pine siding. A pentroof is a piece of trim used with shiplap siding attached at an angle to protect the windows below.

__   2" Heavy, Roughsawn Pine Trim, best for a stain finish.
__   5/4" Cedar Trim, best for a stain finish.
__   5/4" Pine Trim, best for a painted finish

Fascia

The fascia is the trim along the lower edge of the roof. Usually on Yankee Barns it is angled. Alternatively, the roof panels can be cut so the fascia is plumb (at a right angle to the ground), making it easier to install gutters, and giving a more traditional look. If you select traditional trim, the fascia will always be plumb.

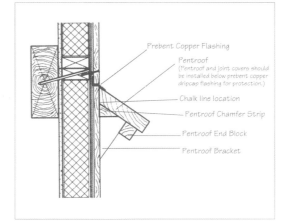

Pentroof

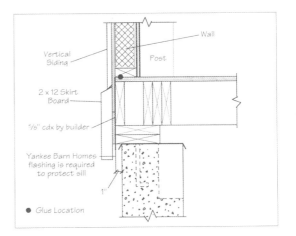

Skirtboard

©Suki Coughlin/ Paula McFarland Stylist

An example of angled fascia

— Angled fascia: At a right angle to the slope of the roof.
— Plumb fascia: At a right angle to the ground.
— Roof Detailing: A 2" drip edge is added to rakes and eaves on the 5/4" trim. This extra detailing provides a more traditional look. The fascia is plumb, and there is a horizontal soffit (the finish board of area underneath the overhang) along the eaves.
— Cornice returns. The fascia and soffit run along the eave side of a roof. The "cornice return" wraps the fascia and soffit around the gable end of the house for a short distance. If you have selected the Traditional style trim, you may want to add cornice returns.

Finish for siding and trim

Having the siding and trim pre-stained or primed protects the wood during construction, and reduces the amount of expensive painting on site. Select whether you want a "semi-solid" stain to let more wood grain show through, or a "solid" stain to give a more paint-like appearance, or just a white primer to paint on site.

Siding:
__ Paint, Color _____
__ Semi-solid stain
__ Solid stain
__ White primer
Trim:
__ Paint, Color _____
__ Semi-solid stain
__ Solid stain
__ White primer

The Roof & Insulation

Innovations in insulation and sealing mean that the magnificent spaces created within a timber frame can be economical and environmentally sound. Homes delivered by Yankee Barn Homes have vented roof panels, which are advantageous because rapid installation on-site protects the timber frame from the weather. Since the panels are supplied with the insulation and the finish ceiling already installed, finishing work on site is reduced (a particular advantage when working on a high cathedral ceiling). The panels have an air space under the plywood top skin to create a vent, which helps prevent ice dams and is required by many shingle manufacturers to help cool roof decks.

Foam roof panels work well with very complex roof shapes, have a slightly higher insulation value, and may be required in some western states where the vented panels have not been approved.

A pre-cut rafter system is useful where there is no timber frame to protect, where a roof is so small or complex that the panels are not efficient, or where high insulating quality may not be so important.

©Suki Coughlin/ Paula McFarland Stylist

An example of plumb fascia.

Windows 101

Windows are a hugely important factor in the appearance of your home, both inside and out, and a major cost factor, too. A lot of thought and planning will go into the windows of your home, as you strive for a uniform appearance, utility, energy efficiency, and longevity.

Yankee Barn Homes supplies wall panels with most of the windows already installed, saving time on site. There is usually a mixture of window styles in each home. The following illustrate the different types of windows. Refer back to this section when choosing window types for the various rooms in your home. Remember, however, that you will probably want consistent styles from an exterior perspective of the home. In other words, for aesthetic reasons, you'll probably want to choose similar styles, symmetrically placed, for the front of your home, and possibly for the side and rear elevations as well.

Double-hung windows slide up and down to open. They are the traditional window style and have the advantage of keeping the sash out of the wind and rain when the window is open. The top and bottom sashes can be cracked to allow for efficient home ventilation during warm weather. A vinyl jamb liner makes it easy to tilt the window into the wash mode.

Casement windows are hinged on one side, and the sash cranks out to open. They are more contemporary looking, and allow more ventilation area than a double hung window. They also allow for a bigger piece of glass for a less obstructed view. Casements seal more tightly since the closed sash is pulled tight against the weather stripping when they are locked. Screens on casements are attached to the inside of the window frame. Because casement windows open out, they are not good for use over a deck or porch, as they will obstruct passage or bump into exterior furnishings.

Awning windows are casement windows that are hinged on the top and crank out to open. These windows create a safety factor in the event of rain.

Gliding windows slide horizontally to open.

Fixed windows are picture windows which are too large to operate, arch windows, or casement or awning size windows that do not operate because they are not accessible.

Specialty windows include fixed windows in circles, arches, or fixed Flexiframe windows in trapezoid, triangle, or other geometric shapes.

Custom 9' Roundtop window is a signature three-unit window made especially for Yankee Barn by Andersen®. The glass is fixed.

Transom windows: A narrow row of glass panes sometimes used above a line of windows, doors, or garage doors. In the case of garage transom windows, they have single thickness glass (non-insulating glass) and a primed wood sash and frame. Barns traditionally used transom windows for lighting, and to keep the fragile window panes out of reach from livestock.

© Andersen® Windows & Doors

A string of casement windows topped by transom windows transforms a dining area into a sunroom.

© Andersen® Windows & Doors

Blank box casement windows crank open, allowing fresh air to inundate a daydreamer's nook.

© Andersen® Windows & Doors

Neat divisions define historic Colonial style in a window, while contemporary manufacture has reserved big open panes for sunlight and view.

Double-hung windows slide up and down. They allow for ventilation both on top and at the bottom. Here, a double-hung window also incorporates a tilt-and-wash feature that eases maintenance.

© Andersen® Windows & Doors

© Andersen® Windows & Doors

Grille work that outlines the panes is typical of Prairie style.

Although you may want to vary your window choices room by room, you will be striving for a thematic exterior appearance. The following is an opportunity for you to express your preferences.

Exterior color for windows:
__ White
__ Sandtone (putty)
__ Terratone® (dark brown)
__ Forest green

Interior color for windows: Interior of the windows is normally left unfinished, so it can be stained or painted on site, and different rooms can have different colors. Windows can alternatively be supplied with a white interior, saving work on site. Note: The sash on casement windows is wrapped with cladding that is the same color as the exterior color. Some of the sash cladding is visible inside the room.
__ Bare wood (clear pine)
__ Prefinished white
__ Primed white for Woodwright® windows only

You may choose to leave your window panes wide open, for a more contemporary look and an unobstructed view. However, for more traditional detailing, you will want to choose a grille system. These grille systems may be permanently applied to the interior and exterior, a system that is more costly, yet more authentic. Removable interior grilles make it much easier to clean the glass, but look less authentic.

__ Removable interior grilles.
__ Removable interior grilles, with permanently applied exterior grille (does not include aluminum spacer in the glass). Tilt-Wash windows have a low-definition exterior grille.
__ Permanently applied interior and exterior grilles, with an aluminum spacer in the glass. Tilt-Wash windows have a low-definition exterior grille.
__ Grille between two panes of glass.

Grille pattern:
__ Colonial
__ Prairie
__ Custom
__ Blank box

Grille widths:
__ 3/4 inch
__ 7/8 inch
__ 1-1/8 inch

You will also need to choose hardware styles for the window cranks, lifts, and locks.

Skylights

Skylights provide light and sometimes ventilation. They can be supplied with a manual control rod to be cranked open, or a motorized control rod, or most conveniently, can be electrically operated by a remote control.

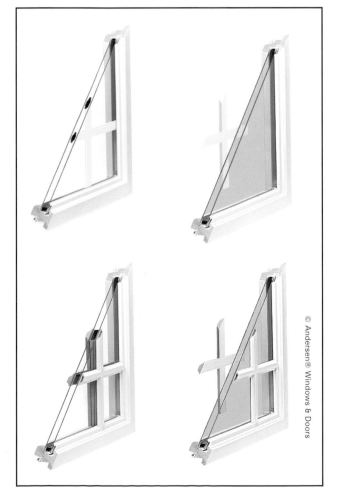

© Andersen® Windows & Doors

Graphics illustrate various grille options for windows.

Doors

A front door serves as a hint of what's beyond. It's the home's primary first impression. It's no mistake that the groom carries a bride over the threshhold of a new home — this is the dramatic entry point to the life indoors. Throughout the home, doors will be placed to generate privacy, block noises, or to protect or conceal property. Generally, the doors throughout a home are fairly uniform in style. The front door, however, is a hallmark of the home, and worth extra thought and planning.

Front doors are generally hinged, but you have many choices throughout the home. Sliding doors, for instance, take up less floor space to operate. Hinged doors may have one or two panels that open, as in the case of French doors. If two panels open, the door is more expensive and you will need to allow adequate wall space for the doors to swing against. Exterior doors generally swing in. Imagine trying to open the door for a visitor and having to push the panel out toward them! Hinged doors that swing out do save floor space, but the open doors must be protected from the weather, and installation of insect screens is difficult. Outswinging doors are usually reserved for use when opening to screened-in porches or other protected areas. Your local building code may dictate the use of fire-safety or steel doors between areas such as the garage or basement and the living areas of the home.

___	Vertical boards
___	Diagonal boards
___	Painted door
___	with screen/storm door
___	without screen/storm door
___	with glass window(s) for view
___	without glass window
___	Sidelight(s)
___	Transom window(s) above

©Suki Coughlin/ Paula McFarland Stylist

Vertical boards create a welcoming front entry door, sandwiched between sidelights and symmetrical lamps.

©Yankee Barn Homes Photo by Rich Frutchey

Inset in a stone wall, double wood doors beckon visitors into an arched nook.

© Andersen® Windows & Doors

A glass door is crowned by transom windows. Because it connects with a back patio, privacy is not an issue.

Porticos were used in each of the three doors on the left to create a focal entryway. The owners' individual styles and personalities are expressed in each case using details such as paint, plants, floor, and platform materials.

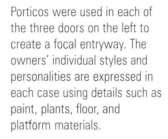

A popular trend in new homes is the two-story foyer. Light from the second floor is admitted up and down in this case, and the first impression is brilliant. Further, this creates a spacious place for the central stairwell. The influx of natural light transforms a place that, by its very nature, tends to be closeted and dark.

These front doors have setbacks that create an approach. The greater the setback, the more impressive the effect. On the other hand, a small setback simply acts as a sheltered lee, where one might get out of the rain while waiting for someone to answer their knock, or where the owners might takc off their shoes before entering.

Simple flagstone steps and a stone stair present a beautiful, humble approach to the home, suggesting that the owners wanted to merge their living quarters with the natural surroundings.

A separate gable has been dedicated to the entryway, with a recessed door to afford shelter to a guest who comes knocking, or the homeowner fumbling for keys. Within, it creates space for stashing shoes and overcoats.

Double doors add ornament to a shingled entry bumpout. The doorway is slightly recessed, allowing the owners a sheltered entry without the cost of a roof overhang or much sacrificed space inside.

Oversized sidelights flank a colorful natural wood door, centerpiece to a symmetrical façade.

Porches

The ultimate retirement plan, the front porch, once furnished with rocking chairs, offers shelter from the rain forever. The front porch is our much imagined respite from work, and even the housework inside. It's where we holler out hellos to our neighbors, and watch the kids cavort on the lawn.

In reality, a porch is simply a floor tucked under a ceiling. Add some decorative railings and you've got a showplace. A porch can be tucked under the same awe-inspiring, rugged timbers that support your home, or you might choose a more economical add-on.

There are three levels of porch construction, in descending order of cost:

1) Roof panels over the post and beam frame. This is a good choice where the porch roof is an extension of the main roof. A vented roof panel system is insulated, which is an advantage if the porch is ever enclosed and heated.

2) Tongue and groove board decking over the post and beam frame.

3) A stick or conventional construction add-on. This is not a good choice if the porch might be enclosed and heated someday.

Construction issues are something your design professional will want to discuss with you if you are seeking a covered porch. You are no doubt more eager to move ahead with furnishing it!

©Yankee Barn Homes Photo by Rich Frutchey

Three dormers and a wrap-around porch define the pretty outline of this country style home.

©Suki Coughlin/ Paula McFarland Stylist

A glorious wrap-around porch hugs the back of this house, capped by an intimate balcony.

Setting a front door in a corner, crowned by glass, creates a unique approach. Log posts add a rustic feel to this entryway.

Soft colors, shady trees, and open railings beckon visitors and family members home.

Enormous picture windows overlook this porch, though the fact is downplayed by mullion or gridwork that preserves a more traditional look. An open feeling is preserved for this entryway, with the two steps leading to the front door greatly distanced, and a bench where one can rest en route.

Beadboard on the porch ceiling has been painted a bright color, and paired with cheerful decor, making this an inviting place for gathering with friends and family.

Decks

A deck is where we barbecue, watch the sun set, and sit out late by lantern light. We position hot tubs here for moonlight soaks. We even garden here, placing containers and creating kitchen gardens and decorative floral displays that can be approached barefoot.

Like porches, decks offer a room outdoors where one can enjoy indoor comfort with a side of fresh air. It's a midway point between nature's forces and man's creature comforts. Independent of roof lines, a deck requires only a door for access in or out. A home can quite easily be completely skirted in decking, or the spaces can be kept intimate, according to the homeowner's lifestyle.

__ Deck to be built with house
__ Deck to be added later

Rooms that will open to a deck:
__ Kitchen
__ Dining Room
__ Living Room
__ Great Room
__ Master Bedroom
__ Other

Board Direction:
__ Diagonal Boards
__ Horizontal
__ Vertical to home

Different directional boards follow the deck as it wraps around the house, encompassing multiple views and serving various rooms of the home.

Planters create a soft, decorative railing for this near-ground level deck.

A corridor of decking leads from the back of the home to the backyard attractions.

A gardener, this homeowner fenced off an area of the deck dedicated to plants.

A big window has a commanding presence over this forest-sheltered deck.

A built-in bench and other furnishings create intimate spaces on a large deck.

A pergola provides partial shade and architectural definition to the home.

An elevated deck wraps around the back of a woodland home.

This expansive, elevated terrace is overlooked by two stories of a paned picture window.

An intimate deck off the master bedroom was built for two, tucked amidst the roofline.

Cushy upholstered furnishings add draw to this backyard retreat.

©Suki Coughlin/ Paula McFarland Stylist

A dramatic staircase was flared and curved, creating a free-standing, wooden ornament for this room.

Now proceed room by room through your home. A survey will help you discuss styles that you prefer. Rather than just checking off your favorite or first choice, you might want to create a ranking system, assigning an "A" to your first choice, "B" to your second. This will help you to set priorities when it comes time to start trimming costs. Working with this list, your designer can help you strike the perfect balance between budget and utopia.

Ceilings

The incredible lengths of wood that form the skeleton of your home can be emphasized or downplayed depending on the way you decorate between the lines. Bright whites contrasted with dark wood finishes will make it stand out more than white panels side-by-side with whitewashed beams. Wood tones on the intermediary panels, likewise, can be coordinated or contrasted.

As you move through the interior shots that follow, study the way beam finishes and ceiling textures and colors work together. The marriages can be combined for any room in your home, and can vary by room if this suits you. As you get to each room, the surveys will include an opportunity to check the style of ceiling finish you prefer.

If you choose boards as your interior finish, they can be factory installed on the bottom of the roof panels, saving work on site. They can be supplied with a sealer or stain, further minimizing work on site. A drywall interior must be finished on site, as well as special painted board finishes.

Eastern White Pine boards can be left rough sawn as they come out of the sawmill. Combined with the naturally knotty appearance of the wood, white pine makes for a more rustic ceiling. The boards are similar to the boards used for the exterior shiplap siding and can be finished in colors similar to those found in siding, or left unfinished and sealed with a clear sealer. White Pine is less expensive than the Southern Yellow Pine, which has few knots and lends itself toward a more formal appearance. Likewise, Southern Yellow Pine can be finished in white or with a clear sealer.

Additionally, ceilings can be finished in blue board or gypsum for a smooth, plaster-type finish. Particle board or plywood will be used if you choose a custom finish, such as a herringbone pattern of angled boards or stucco finish.

All or most rooms will have the following finish:

__ Eastern White Pine, rough sawn and knotty
    __ white finish
    __ clear sealer
__ Southern Yellow Pine
    __ white
    __ clear sealer
__ Plaster veneer
__ Other (stucco, herringbone boards, etc.)

Floors

The choices of flooring are as varied as the imagination, spanning from bamboo to vinyl. In our survey, we've simply included the most popular and/or common choices. As you work room by room, feel free to pen in some creative alternatives if they appeal to you.

Main Entry

This is the place where people will form their very first impression upon entering the home, and modify any assumptions they made from the outside. We greet our loved ones and friends here, and extend our welcome. Here is a place where you present the opportunity to travel to the more public or private areas of the home.

Your family may or may not use this entrance. It's as likely that they will enter from the garage, or through a mudroom on the side of the house. The entryway may, however, double as stairwell, and thus the passageway to bedrooms, baths, and other private areas.

Following are some questions that will help you distill your vision for the entryway or foyer of your home.

©Suki Coughlin/ Paula McFarland Stylist

___ The front door should be reached via a covered porch.

___ A foyer is necessary.

___ Impressive impact for visitors is important.

___ A two-story foyer is desirable.

___ A custom front door and/or transoms and sidelights are desirable.

___ The home's post and beam structure should be visible from the foyer

___ Frequent guests, or the family's regular use of the front door, make a coat closet imperative.

___ As in many traditional homes, the staircase should be located in the entryway.

___ Family members will usually use a side, back, or garage entrance to the home.

___ Family areas should be concealed from view via the main entryway.

___ Family areas can be visible from the entryway.

Rooms adjacent:
___ Powder room
___ Dining room
___ Living room
___ Family Room/Great Room
___ Home office

Flooring
___ Wide plank (pine)
___ Hardwood
___ Tile
___ Stone
___ Other

Stairs

A staircase is like a stage for the home. Imagine the many movies where the staircase has acted as conduit for great entrances, exits, or pivotal turning points.

Though not often thought of, the staircase is a critical component of the home. Obviously it is the means of getting from one level to another. Placement of the staircase dictates a great deal of traffic flow through the home, and can make accessing different floors of the home convenient or a general nuisance depending on the home's layout. Several emotional or lifestyle factors play a role in determining where a staircase will be placed. In many cases, homeowners elect to place the staircase in the foyer, a reassuringly traditional location. Also, by having sleeping quarters feed directly to a door, one facilitates a rapid evacuation in the event of a fire!

In some cases, however, as in the case of a couple who entertain often, and yet want the children to be able to play and watch TV in family areas, the staircase may be located away from greeting, dining, and formal areas of the home. The same goes for the homeowner who conducts business in the home.

Stairs are challenging in home design because the designer needs to think both vertically and horizontally, and find room — stairs take up a lot of space. Therefore they are one of the first things a designer will place within the floor plan. For starters, stairs need to be designed to have proper headroom under the ceiling so the stairs do not end under a sloped ceiling that is less than six feet, eight inches high. This, obviously, dictates placement. Stairs are generally located in the center of the home, or along the eave wall.

It is more difficult to fit center stairs straight into buildings that are less than twenty-five feet wide. Remember, too, that stairs need landings — at least three feet, three inches square minimum — to provide access to other living areas. Stairs in the entry need to be four to five feet from doors and walls. A staircase is at least three feet, six inches wide. As

©Yankee Barn Homes Photo by Rich Frutchey

ceilings get taller you need more steps and risers, and each step adds ten inches more to the length of the stair case.

You may or may not want to concern yourself with the technical aspects of stair location and construction. What is important to you and your lifestyle is location. As mentioned above, the entryway is traditionally home to the staircase, but you may wish to limit your long walks from the family room at the back of the home, to the front stairway, to your bedroom at the back of the home. Locating your stair-set in the center third of the home will reduce long walks. Wherever you place it, you will probably want to save space and locate your basement stairs below the main stairway.

Your aesthetics will also be considered when configuring the stairs. Stairs are most often straight, L-shaped, or U-shaped. The length of a typical straight stair is eleven feet. The length of a typical U-shaped stair is eight feet. The U-shape along the eave allows better division of the building space. The length of a typical L-shaped stair is thirteen feet. This layout allows the stair to bend around other areas, such as a powder room or storage space. A circular staircase creates an elegant look, and is a wonderful way to access lofts and other little-used places. However, it is not practical for regular traffic, nor universally accessible for elderly or very young family members.

Placement
    __ Front of house/by entryway
    __ In the back for private upstairs access
    __ Multiple stairways
Shape
    __ L-shaped
    __ U-shaped
    __ Curved
    __ Circular staircase to loft area
Stair material
    __ Wood
    __ Carpeted
    __ Other
Railing
    __ Standard wood vertical balusters
    __ Wrought iron
    __ Other

©Yankee Barn Homes Photo by Rich Frutchey

An L-shaped staircase was left open, allowing for an artful display.

©2003 F&E Schmidt

A straight shot upstairs, this staircase shares billing with a narrow hallway.

©Suki Coughlin/ Paula McFarland Stylist

An L-shaped central staircase includes a platform. This dramatic midway point between upstairs and down serves as a convenient, central communication center.

©Yankee Barn Homes Photo by Rich Frutchey

Closet space can be tucked under a U-shaped staircase

The Kitchen

The kitchen is called the heart of the home. With the exception of bedrooms, it is often the most used. Here is where we generate a lot of happy memories, of moments gathered around the kitchen table, or baking cookies with grandmom.

Because you're building a post and beam home, there are few restrictions on how your kitchen will be configured. Free of inside support walls, you are only limited by your desires and what makes you feel most comfortable. You may find, after looking at enough kitchen images, that you prefer a more traditonal gathering place for your clan, or that you like the idea of being sequestered in a removed work space for food preparation.

Kitchen designers recommend that this room be designed around the "work triangle," keeping the refrigerator, sink, and stovetop all within easy turning distance. It is also important to position the dishwasher near the sink, and to keep the microwave oven in a handy place. The following checklist is a good place to start when you approach a kitchen designer to work out details for your cabinetry. If you and your partner agree on these basic decisions, you've overcome the major obstacles a designer faces in creating your dream kitchen. Visiting a kitchen showroom, or ordering catalog information from major cabinet manufacturers is a good way to compare and choose cabinet styles that suit you.

The basic kitchen footprints or configurations are as follows. Check the style or styles that most appeal to you.

©Yankee Barn Homes Photo by Rich Frutchey

Pendant lighting, skylights and an impressive range hood lead the eye up in this open, airy kitchen. The cabinetry was kept primarily under a lovely black granite counter.

©Yankee Barn Homes Photo by Rich Frutchey

A craftsman style kitchen is defined by the tidy, squared-off glass-front cabinets. A center island doubles as cook space and a raised eating counter, putting the chef in the spotlight. The homeowner has accessorized with red, adding warmth to the room.

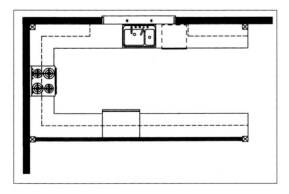

__ Galley: an aisleway room with appliances and countertops on two sides of a passageway. A Galley kitchen has what looks like a corridor running through it. The work triangle can be short. This arrangement is most often used in a guesthouse or apartment.

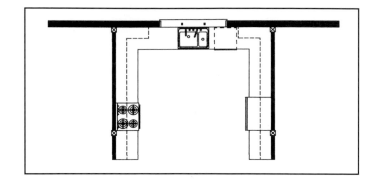

A U-shaped kitchen, possibly with a peninsula, is quite efficient. The work triangle tends to be short and the space usage small. This arrangement works well for a one-person kitchen.

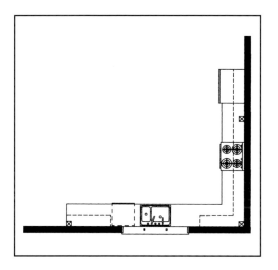

An L-shaped kitchen is created with two walls at right angles. The work triangle is longer than in the U-shaped or Island kitchen. In a corner kitchen, appliances and countertops are arranged along two walls. An island often forms the opposing corner, offering an eating area or food prep area that faces into other parts of the home.

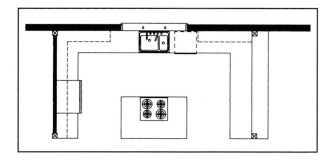

Island kitchen in which an island sits between two walls or a horseshoe of appliances and countertops. This requires a larger kitchen. An Island kitchen lengthens the work triangle, but affords the convenience of an extra surface on which to place food and dishes.

©Suki Coughlin/ Paula McFarland Stylist

Blue cabinetry defines the kitchen area, tucked under a loft, yet part of a larger room beyond. Two sinks create an opportunity for one person to work at the island, another by the windows.

©Yankee Barn Homes Photo by Rich Frutchey

Wood and white tones create a country style craftsman's kitchen. Enormous picture windows embrace the view.

©Suki Coughlin/ Paula McFarland Stylist

This kitchen is an excellent example of partial framing. The granary, or extension under the slant roof, has no timber frame support.

Estimated room size of kitchen: _____

Kitchen to include:
__ Eat-in kitchen with room for table and (#)__ chairs
__ Island counter with stool seating, (#)__ stools
__ Adjacent breakfast nook with room for table and (#)__ chairs
__ Post and beam structure is apparent.
__ Dry wall finish
__ Raised ceiling to match living areas beyond
__ Lowered ceiling to create more intimate work/ congregation area

Flooring
__   Wide plank (pine)
__   Hardwood
__   Tile
__   Stone
__   Other

©Yankee Barn Homes Photo by Rich Frutchey

A large island creates enormous counter space, as well as an informal dining area in an open kitchen/great room.

One wall of this kitchen has been dedicated to the view, so the cook never feels trapped in her duties.

©Suki Coughlin/ Paula McFarland Stylist

Outside window: __ Yes __ No
__ Double-hung windows
__ Casement windows
__ Awning window
__ Gliding window
__ Fixed or picture window
__ Specialty window

Rooms adjacent:
__ Mudroom/laundry
__ Dining room
__ Outside deck
__ Family Room/Great Room
__ Breakfast nook

Cabinetry
__ Wood stained to match post and beams
__ White
__ Painted or laminate
__ Color-stained wood

Countertop
__ Granite/stone
__ Solid surface
__ Butcher block
__ Tile
__ Laminate
__ Other (concrete, stainless steel, ...)

Appliances:
Color Preference:
__ Stainless steel
__ Black
__ White
Refrigerator
__ Side-by-side
__ Stacked
__ Undercounter beverage cooler

A bumpout roofline extends the kitchen to a picture window work area. Within, cabinetry space is maximized under the counters and with a set of overhead cabinets suspended from a beam.

Stools act as a visitor center for the chef, who labors within a wealth of countertop work area.

A picture window is a nice termination for the far side of a U-shaped kitchen.

The kitchen opens directly to a deck, for quick *al fresco* dinners.

Yellow cabinetry adds sunshine to an inviting U-shaped kitchen.

Oven
  __ Wall mounted
  __ Undercounter
Stovetop
  __ With oven unit
  __ Separate range
  __ Four burners
  __ Six burners
  __ Gas
  __ Electric
Stove ventilation
  __ Hood
  __ Downdraft
Microwave Oven
  __ Wall mounted
  __ Countertop unit
  __ Undercounter
Sink
  __ One basin
  __ Two basins
  __ Farmer's sink
Backsplash
  __ Laminate
  __ Tile

Other uses:

  __   Desk area
  __   Computer center/internet access
  __   Phone
  __   Television

Pantry

A kitchen pantry or butler's pantry is a wonderful luxury. Food, small appliances, and bulk supplies can be tucked away, eliminating the need for much of the kitchen cabinetry. Pantries are becoming an increasingly popular asset as more and more homeowners choose to open their kitchens to other living areas, eliminating walls that would house cabinets. If you've opted to design a pantry into your home plan, which type do you prefer:

  __   Walk-in
  __   Closet size
  __   Cabinet unit with fold out shelves and racks
  __   Wire shelves
  __   Wood shelves

A breakfast nook area has been created just beyond the kitchen work areas. An island houses the cooktop, and abuts one of the home's supportive posts.

An eat-in kitchen competes with a sunroom dining area just beyond. The kitchen table doubles as island workspace, and multiplies the countertop area many fold.

Posts and beam add country flavor to this kitchen, which is strong on wood accents.

An expanse of floor space can be a luxury when young ones want to play in the same room where the cook is working.

Teddy holds a place for a precious grandchild. The U-shaped kitchen was kept open to the rest of the house, allowing visual access but encouraging non-working visitors to congregate on the other side of the barrier.

An informal dining area spans the space between kitchen and living room in an open floor plan.

Green cabinetry dares to be different. Open shelves and a wealth of windows create a wide-open impression. Storage space was kept below counters to maximize the effect of the tall ceiling.

Contrasts in white against dark beams emphasize the beauty of the structure.

A kitchen is tucked off a
passageway between
living and dining areas.

©Suki Coughlin/ Paula McFarland Stylist

©Yankee Barn Homes

Skylights emphasize the soaring slant of the kitchen ceiling.

A tile-counter tops an island work station/breakfast nook. An overhead beam does double-duty as chandelier.

A kitchen area is tucked below the loft, just off the great room of the home.

Beams were used to define
different zones within this
soaring space.

©Yankee Barn Homes Photo by Paul Jeremias

A conventional ceiling with
pocket lamps provides a
familiar sense of place in this
all-American kitchen.

©Suki Coughlin/ Paula McFarland Stylist

Colorful accents and a mix of dark and
light cabinetry lend a casual, playful
tone to this small kitchen space.

©Yankee Barn Homes Photo by Rich Frutchey

A galley kitchen creates a passageway. In this modern, post and beam twist, one wall has been left open to the home beyond for significantly different effect.

©Yankee Barn Homes Photo by Ross Chapple

A compact work area minimizes the number of steps required to complete tasks in the kitchen. Here, sink and stove are but a step away.

Courtesy of House Beautiful's Building Manual; ©1985 by the Hearst Corp.

Open shelving both above and below the counter, plus a wall of pots and pans, perfect the "old farm" feel of this rustic home.

An overhead hood ventilates the range below, and provides lighting. Wood panels conceal the side-by-side refrigerator beyond, coordinating them with the cabinetry.

Brick is a wonderful accent for a kitchen/dining area, here housing a warm wood stove that proves very useful, and popular, during winter months.

A blue-gray finish on the cabinetry creates a ground line in a soaring space.

Breakfast Nooks

In any home that can afford the space, day-to-day dining areas are separate from the formal "dining room." In many cases, this takes the form of a nook. Usually a small area set aside from food preparation areas, the nook functions as part of the kitchen, but separate.

©Yankee Barn Homes Photo by Rich Frutchey

Estimated room size: _____
__ Room for table and (#)__ chairs

__ Post and beam structure is apparent
__ Raised ceiling to match living areas beyond
__ Lowered ceiling to create a more intimate area
__ Sunroom with glass walls/ceiling or maximized windows and skylights

Flooring
__ Wide plank (pine)
__ Hardwood
__ Tile
__ Stone
__ Other

Outside window
__ Yes
__ No
__ Double-hung windows
__ Casement windows
__ Awning window
__ Gliding windows
__ Fixed or picture window
__ Specialty window

©Suki Coughlin/ Paula McFarland Stylist

Above: Tucked amidst windows, this beautiful brick-floored breakfast nook offers a sunny start to the day. Left: Likewise, a greenhouse addition creates a favorite gathering place, be it for meals or leisurely escapes with the newspaper and a cup of coffee.

A sunroom addition doubles as breakfast nook.

A potbellied stove warms both a sitting area and a breakfast nook, in a sunny extension of the kitchen.

In both of the images above, an extended counter doubles as a breakfast nook, with barstool seating.

Formal Dining Room

Many homes today eschew a formal dining room, instead having a large table in the kitchen. Generally, a formal dining room is an enclosed area that includes a table that can be extended to accommodate major gatherings. It may also be furnished with a china cabinet, for the good china and silverware, and a buffet, where foods are placed for serving. Though seldom used, it is an expected house asset, and may be critical to selling your home in the future. Some people design a dining room with alternate uses. For instance, custom shelving may be included to make the room double as a library. A desk can make the room double as a home office center, or homework station.

A small dining room might be ten feet by twelve feet. A medium size dining room might be fifteen feet by seventeen feet. Start by measuring your current dining room and dining table. Work from these figures in determining if you want more or less space for your dining area.

The following are considerations for designing your formal dining room.

Estimated room size: _____
___   Seating for (#)__ people
___   Buffet/sideboard
___   China cabinet/hutch
___   Fireplace

Siting
___   Deck access
___   Four walls (concealed from other rooms)
___   French doors to divide from other areas of the home
___   Fireplace
___   Adjacent to kitchen
___   Adjacent to foyer
___   Adjacent to formal living room
___   Adjacent to great room
___   Part of great room

©Keith Scott Morton

Timber framework provides a setting for formal dining. The dining room is connected to the kitchen by a buffet counter and glass-front cabinets.

©Brad Simmons

Windsor chairs and a big sideboard are wonderful antique accents for this spacious dining area.

General Appearance

— Post and beam structure is apparent.
— Drywall finish
— Paneled with custom built-ins
— Chair rail
— Wainscoting (paneling below the chair rail)
— Raised ceiling to match living areas beyond
— Lowered ceiling to create more intimate area

Flooring

— Hardwood
— Wide plank pine
— Other

Outside window: __ Yes __ No

— Double-hung windows
— Casement windows
— Awning windows
— Gliding windows
— Fixed or picture window
— Specialty window

©Yankee Barn Homes Photo by Rich Frutchey

Top: Coordinating burgundy half-wall and carpet define the dining area between an arts and crafts kitchen and comfortable sitting area.
Right: A table-side fireplace provides fuel and motivation to linger after the meal.

©Suki Coughlin/ Paula McFarland Stylist

The wrought iron candelabra heightens a sense of history in this room. Wood lovers, the owners have filled the room with natural-finish furnishings, flooring, and, of course, architectural beams.

©Suki Coughlin/ Paula McFarland Stylist

China adds appropriate ornament to the
mantel of a dining room fireplace.

Rich, warm colors and upholstered chairs add to the comfort
of a formal dining room.

Carpet and carpentry help to
define the formal dining area
within a great room.

Architecture is among the artwork on display in this sunny, soaring dining area. A chandelier provides wonderful lighting after the sun sets.

An antique hutch and country style chairs set a casual tone for this open dining area.

Brickwork and an elaborate Oriental carpet create color and excitement in this open dining area.

Casement windows connect both kitchen countertop and the dining table beyond with the home's best feature, the view.

A sunroom extension defines the boundaries of a formal dining area. Asian wicker works with the dark stain in adding a sense of the exotic.

Neatly tucked behind the chimney, a dining room feels secluded yet connected to other areas of the home. Most importantly, the cook is still in contact with her guests while they are seated.

Stencil work and floral motifs reveal the hand of a
woman in decorating this country pine dining area.

A trio of traditional, small-paned windows add to the historic feel of this
room. Windsor chairs and a corner hutch are wonderful antique additions to
new home construction.

The typical American home has a formal dining area reserved at the
front of the house for special occasions. Unused, it is usually a nice stop
on the tour, with the table clear of clutter, the shelves tidy.

Great Room

The hottest trend in contemporary housing, the great room rolls living, family, television, dining, and often kitchens all into one expansive space. Focused around a central fireplace, or a wall of windows and decking, the great room creates an irresistible magnet where family members and guests gather. In timber frame homes, this room often extends up to the roof, and links with upstairs bedrooms via a loft — putting the entire home in communication. It can be tucked off into an ell of the home, making it a private family place, or sit smack dab in the middle, opening up as part of a guest's first impression of the place upon entering.

Great rooms located in the gable end of a house are most cost effective. Center great rooms work well when the great room wants to be the center of all activity and the view is on the eaves side of the house (center great rooms use a large multistoried dormer or a bump out dormer). Great rooms can also be located in an ell, which is the most expensive option because the structure is one story.

Timber frame construction makes a great room possible, and makes it beautiful. Here, beams define this enormous family space, framing doorways, fireplace, and the lofty vistas above.

©Yankee Barn Homes Photo by Paul Jeremias

Siting
__ Center of home
__ In private ell
__ Contains kitchen
__ Adjacent to kitchen
__ Contains dining room
__ Adjacent to dining room
__ Contains formal living room
__ Adjacent to formal living room
__ Adjacent to Foyer
__ Deck access

General Appearace
__ Post and beam structure is apparent.
__ Dry wall finish
__ Raised ceiling to match living areas beyond
__ Visual access to second floor/loft area
__ Fireplace

Flooring
__ Wide plank (pine)
__ Hardwood
__ Tile
__ Carpet
__ Other

Outside window: __ Yes __ No
__ Double-hung windows
__ Casement windows
__ Awning windows
__ Gliding windows
__ Fixed or picture window
__ Specialty window
__ 9-foot roundtop window

Furnishings (indicate how many)
__ Couch
__ Loveseat
__ Upholstered Chair
__ Ottoman
__ Desk
__ Television
__ Bookcases
__ Other

©Brad Simmons

A coffee table doubles as dining space in a room interconnected with the kitchen, as well as lofty overlooks from the upper floors. An exposed chimney creates a great stone barrier between the living area and a room on the other side, while still allowing oral communication.

A fireplace forms the focal point, grounding the focus under a soaring cathedral ceiling.

©Brad Simmons

Furnishings should match the scale of the room, as does the impressive armoire on the far wall. Stately furniture lends formality to this space.

©Suki Coughlin/ Paula McFarland Stylist

A two-story window emphasizes the height of this soaring great room. It also filters light to a second floor loft beyond the open railing.

©Suki Coughlin/ Paula McFarland Stylist

A round-top window caps a 9-foot wide tower of mullioned glass. The effect is unforgetable.

©Suki Coughlin/ Paula McFarland Stylist

Here, window panes were left open for an unadulterated connection with the leaves and deck beyond.

A loft captures some of the upper air within this soaring great room. Note how the flooring was stained to match the timbers.

Below, furniture is positioned to give equal billing to a massive fireplace and an almost shadow-like shape of windows and inviting French doors on the next wall. Bottom right: Brick forms the central focal point for a two-story great room, connected visually with the kitchen and a loft area.

French doors fold open invitingly beneath a towering, round-top window. The wall of glass floods the open space with natural light.

Light colored furnishings paired with white finish on walls and V-groove ceiling help to emphasize the soaring nature of this room and accentuate the wooden beams.

A collection of finds from around the world create an exotic aura in this great room.

Fireplaces

You may want a great big hearth in your great room. As a central focal place of the home, this is one piece of the home on which you'll lavish lots of thought. Towering, two-story chimneys are popular.

Contemporary innovations allow you to install a propane pipeline and enjoy fire at the flick of a switch, and to extinguish the fire just as quickly. A double-sided fireplace can allow two rooms to enjoy the fireplace simultaneously — a family area and the dining room, for instance.

Placement is critical, both aesthetically and for the health of the home. A stone column on the exterior of the home is an attractive architectural feature. On the other hand, keeping the fireplace near an outside wall is very useful when you are hauling wood in to feed it. Located near sliding or French doors on the deck, messy wood doesn't need to travel through your home enroute to the flames.

A fireplace may be merely decorative, or it may serve as an alternate or main source of heat for the home. In the case of many woodstoves, pellet stoves, and even some fireplaces, fuel use is very efficient. Plus, fire-generated heat is cozy, and beyond compare in visual appeal.

A fireplace is an emotional touchstone for your home. Even though the average hearth owner uses their fireplace less than twice a year, studies find that it is very difficult to sell a home without one. Be sure to lavish plenty of attention on making the main fireplace — and any other fireplaces you provide in your home — perfect.

The first thing and the last thing you see in a room is the fireplace. Furnishings are arranged in homage to the hearth. Here the hearth is decorated, always on display even when it's not on fire.

A mantel is made of the same great wood that frames the home, integrating the stone with the structure itself.

©Yankee Barn Homes Photo by Rich Frutchey

Siting
__ Great Room
__ Living Room
__ Family Room
__ Kitchen
__ Dining Room
__ Master Bedroom
__ Other

(If more than one, indicate room: Great Room – G; Living Room – L, etc.)
__ Wood burning fireplace
__ Gas fireplace
__ Woodstove
__ Pellet stove
__ Other

General Appearance
__ Exposed stone chimney
__ Concealed chimney
__ Fieldstone
__ River (round) stones
__ Cut stone
__ Simulated stone (concrete)
__ Brick
__ Tile
__ Other

Mantel
__ Same material as chimney
__ Wood ledge
__ Wood surround
__ Other

A cap stone creates an impressive focal point just above the fire, part of an admirable example of stone construction. Far right: Irregular granite block is crowned by a wooden beam, with a drywall finished chimney above.

©Yankee Barn Homes Photo by Rich Frutchey

©Yankee Barn Homes Photo by Rich Frutchey

©Suki Coughlin/ Paula McFarland Stylist

©Suki Coughlin/ Paula McFarland Stylist

©Suki Coughlin/ Paula McFarland Stylist

©Yankee Barn Homes Photo by Rich Frutchey

©Suki Coughlin/ Paula McFarland Stylist

©Suki Coughlin/ Paula McFarland Stylist

©Suki Coughlin/ Paula McFarland Stylist

©Suki Coughlin/ Paula McFarland Stylist

©Suki Coughlin/ Paula McFarland Stylist

©Suki Coughlin/ Paula McFarland Stylist

©Yankee Barn Homes

©Yankee Barn Homes Photo by Ross Chapple

©Suki Coughlin/ Paula McFarland Stylist

©Suki Coughlin/ Paula McFarland Stylist

©Yankee Barn Homes Photo by Paul Jeremias

Formal Living Room

This room is often the showplace of the home. A family may only use it once a year, at Christmas time. Or they may put it to use frequently for formal entertaining. It is rare to find a television in a living room, though there are no rules against it. The following checklist will help your designer ensure that your living room presents the appropriate statement.

Approximate size: _____

Furnishings (indicate how many)
- __ Couch
- __ Loveseat
- __ Upholstered Chair
- __ Ottoman
- __ Desk
- __ Piano

Siting
- __ Faces front of home
- __ Opens off foyer
- __ Opens off dining room
- __ Fireplace

General Appearance
- __ Post and beam structure is apparent
- __ Dry wall finish
- __ Raised ceiling to match living areas beyond
- __ Lowered ceiling to create more intimate area

Flooring
- __ Wide plank (pine)
- __ Hardwood
- __ Tile
- __ Carpet

Outside window: __ Yes __ No
- __ Double-hung windows
- __ Casement windows
- __ Awning windows
- __ Gliding windows
- __ Fixed or picture window
- __ Specialty window

©Suki Coughlin/ Paula McFarland Stylist

Dark timbers contribute to the more intimate environment in this family room.

©Suki Coughlin/ Paula McFarland Stylist

Wood and stone work together to add warmth to this intimate setting.

A striped sofa adds a softening effect to the formal antique furnishings in this sun-soaked sitting parlor.

A sunroom takes on a formal air, with crisp white furnishings arranged perpendicular to walls.

Reality Check

Who will use this room?
How many hours a week will you spend
    here?
Will you use it during the daytime,
    nighttime, or both?
Will you entertain here?

Furnishings help establish the formal nature of a living room. Here wooden legs on the upholstered furniture, and ornate window treatments add style and elegance.

Mullioned windows add classical appeal to a simply furnished room. Upright seating contributes to the formal feeling in this firelit sitting area.

Family Room/Media Room

Perhaps you are creating this room in lieu of or in addition to a great room. The family room is generally a quiet place, often referred to as a den. Here family members may read or curl up in front of the television together. More than likely you'll want it located at the back of the home.

Approximate size: _____

Furnishings (indicate how many)
___ Couch
___ Loveseat
___ Upholstered Chair
___ Ottoman
___ Desk
___ Television
___ Bookshelves
___ Other
___ Fireplace

Siting
___ Faces backyard
___ Opens off kitchen
___ Opens off dining room

General Appearance
___ Post and beam structure is apparent.
___ Dry wall finish
___ Raised ceiling to match living areas beyond
___ Standard 8-foot ceiling

Flooring
___ Wide plank (pine)
___ Hardwood
___ Tile
___ Carpet

Outside window: __ Yes __ No
___ Double-hung windows
___ Casement windows
___ Awning windows
___ Gliding windows
___ Fixed or picture window
___ Specialty window

©2003 F&E Schmidt

A library is furnished with comfy chairs and a warm fireplace, creating a favorite hangout for family members.

©2003 F&E Schmidt

Windows extend from knee-high to near the ceiling, offering an unadulterated view whether the occupants are sitting or standing.

An open stone fireplace offers seating on both sides, and a peekaboo opportunity between rooms.

©Suki Coughlin/ Paula McFarland Stylist

Whether you're one of those lucky individuals who actually works out of the home, or if you simply want a place where the kids can do homework and the family finances can be coordinated, a home office is a wonderful luxury. More and more homes include these bonus rooms. They are often rich in custom paneling and shelving, and reminiscent of the male bastion, where gentlemen would retire after dinner for a cigar and talk of business. If this is truly a place where you will conduct business, you might want to locate it immediately off the foyer, so that business guests need not intrude on the life of the family beyond.

Approximate size: _____

Furnishings (indicate how many)
___ Couch
___ Loveseat
___ Upholstered chair
___ Ottoman
___ Desk
___ Swivel chair

General Appearance
___ Post and beam structure is apparent.
___ Drywall finish
___ Paneled with custom built-ins
___ Chair rail
___ Wainscoting (paneling below the chair rail)
___ Raised ceiling to match living areas beyond
___ Lowered ceiling for more intimate area
___ Fireplace

Flooring
___ Wide plank (pine)
___ Hardwood
___ Tile
___ Carpet

Siting
___ Deck access
___ Four walls (concealed from other rooms)
___ French doors to divide from other areas of the home
___ Adjacent to dining room
___ Adjacent to foyer
___ Adjacent to formal living room
___ Adjacent to great room
___ Part of great room
___ Upstairs or spare bedroom

Outside window: ___ Yes ___ No
___ Double-hung windows
___ Casement windows
___ Awning windows
___ Gliding windows slide horizontally to open
___ Fixed or picture window
___ Specialty window

©Suki Coughlin/ Paula McFarland Stylist

A handsome round-top window adds light and inspiration to a writer's work area.

©Yankee Barn Homes Photo by Sidney Morris

The view helps keep a worker at his desk.

Sunroom/Greenhouse

Maybe you're looking for a sunny room that doubles as breakfast nook or family room. Or maybe you want a full-fledged greenhouse or spa room, with a glass roof angled for all-day sun exposure. Skylights are another option, creating a way to let the sun shine in while saving costs and skirting the technical challenges of constructing glass walls and ceilings.

Glass traces the sides and slopes of these bumpout sunrooms, both serving as breakfast nooks.

A board ceiling caps a screened-in porch.

©Suki Coughlin/ Paula McFarland Stylist

©Yankee Barn Homes Photo by Sidney Morris

©Suki Coughlin/ Paula McFarland Stylist

French doors and sliding windows team up to create a glass-encompassed sunroom.

©Suki Coughlin/ Paula McFarland Stylist

An expanse of angled glass completes the eave over this lengthy dining area.

©Suki Coughlin/ Paula McFarland Stylist

A small, glass bumpout provides a petite retreat off the dining area.

Master Bedroom

The most personal of rooms, the master bedroom is where you must feel safe. Here your worries are put aside and you rest, literally. It is an intimate space, where few venture besides the brief glimpse of a fifty-cent tour.

Master bedrooms can be located in the main house or in ells. The considerations are usually size and privacy requirements. The main house location is generally more economical than an ell or wing. Maybe you want a suite, with room for a sitting area where you might read, watch TV, or share morning cups of coffee. Or maybe you'll simply sleep here, and want to save your living space for other areas of the house.

Again, it helps to measure your current accommodations and work from there. Do you plan to take the same furnishings with you?

Approximate size: _____

Furnishings (indicate how many)
__   Double or queen bed
__   King size bed
__   High dresser
__   Low dresser
__   Vanity
__   Couch
__   Love seat
__   Upholstered chair
__   Ottoman
__   Settee
__   Table

Siting
__   First floor of main house (typically has flat ceiling)
__   Second floor of main house (typically has cathedral ceiling)
__   Ell (single story)
__   Wing (two story)
__   Back of the house
__   Limited windows for privacy
__   Picture windows to maximize view
__   Private deck

General Appearance
__   Post and beam structure is apparent.
__   Dry wall finish
__   Raised ceiling
__   Lowered ceiling
__   Fireplace

Flooring
__   Wide plank (pine)
__   Hardwood
__   Carpet

Outside window: __ Yes __ No
__   Double-hung windows
__   Casement windows
__   Awning windows
__   Gliding windows slide horizontally to open.
__   Fixed or picture window
__   Specialty window

©Yankee Barn Homes Photo by Rich Frutchey

Four posters rise amidst the rafters.

Closets

You may want to have conventional closets with two doors or walk-in style. Many new homes incorporate his and her closets or one large walk-in divided into two spaces.

A walk-in closet may only need one door where twelve feet of normal closet uses four doors.

The master bedroom can easily use twelve to eighteen linear feet of actual clothes hanging space and other bedrooms can use six to eight feet.

Walk-in closets should be at least five feet wide for L-shape closets and seven feet wide for U-shape closets.

Closets should be at least two feet deep. The average bedroom closet is two feet deep and six to seven feet long.

__(#)   Regular room closets will suffice
__(#)   Walk-in closets

©Suki Coughlin/ Paula McFarland Stylist

Blue and white combine for classic country style appeal in both of these master suites.

©2003 F&E Schmidt

A little natural light was desired to assist in the waking process, but these homeowners placed more emphasis on the soothing glow of a fire in their bedroom.

Rose and cream tones blend for a warm and inviting place, perfect for hunkering down at night by the roaring woodstove, great for stretching awake in the glow of picture windows and glass French doors.

A master suite opens directly to a private deck, for those who prefer to take their morning toast with the birds.

A bedroom doubles as sunroom, with windows flanking three sides. Curtains circle the bed for privacy or dimming when desired.

A panel of artful foliage set between white-stained beams presents a contemporary look for this sleek master suite.

Ribbons, flowers, and a feminine writing desk bear the mistress's mark.

The wooded backyard is as close as sliding glass doors.

Wood doors, heavy beams, brick and stone
fireplace, and a low ceiling work together to create
a sense of history in this new home.

Just because a house was built of timber frame, it doesn't mean the bedroom has to have huge slabs of timber running through it. These homeowners opted for a more standard look.

A wonderful wall of glass connects the masters of the house with their wooded environment. Strong support timbers make this flimsy connection possible.

The ceiling itself is art for this room, outlined in dark beams. In addition to the French door, transoms, and sidelights, natural light is admitted through small sidewall windows.

An eight-foot ceiling creates a grounded feeling for a bedroom where the owners didn't think they'd feel comfortable with too much space above their heads.

A large, floral-print wallpaper is a pleasing effect between timbers and a round-top window. The crochet covered bed is placed for a maximum view of the lake beyond.

A ceiling fan and spacious ceilings limit the need for air conditioning on all but the hottest of nights.

Rich, natural tones create a more masculine feel for this room, dominated by a big round-top window.

Beams define the central roofline, along with a dormer. The effect is mesmerizing. The homeowners left the focus on the beams, eschewing window treatments and wall art. Below right: Though not structurally necessary, these beams were chosen to impart the feel of post and beam construction. For privacy in the ground-floor bedroom, the owners curtained their windows three-quarters of the way up.

©Yankee Barn Homes Photo by Rich Frutchey

©Suki Coughlin/ Paula McFarland Stylist

©Suki Coughlin/ Paula McFarland Stylist

A fireplace is a wonderful, romantic addition to a bedroom suite. This one was planned large enough to house a loveseat and chairs, affording a conversation area for the masters of the house.

©2003 F&E Schmidt

Above right: Supportive beams crisscross this room and coordinate with a timber bedframe. Tudor effect is created using a dark stain in contrast with white walls and ceiling. Bottom right: A four-poster bed points to the cathedral ceiling. A private deck and a massive picture window make this room a place where dreams truly are inspired.

©Suki Coughlin/ Paula McFarland Stylist

Courtesy of House Beautiful's Building Manual; ©1985 by the Hearst Corp.

A wealth of white adds a clean, fresh feeling to a master suite
where one can freshen up in a whirlpool tub bedside!

©Brad Simmons

Tucked under a gambrel roof, a master suite opens
to a private balcony. A chaise lounge at the foot of
the bed takes advantage of the view.

©Yankee Barn Homes Photo by Ross Chapple

A feminine hand added ornament and style to this
impressive suite. The effect is richly exotic. Support
columns help to define the sleeping and dressing
areas from the whirlpool tub beyond.

©Suki Coughlin/ Paula McFarland Stylist

A mountain view was paramount to the design of this second-floor master
bedroom and balcony. The timbered space simply reconfirms the soaring sky

Master Bath

This is a room you use every day. You may not linger here, you may wish you could. Primarily for cleansing and pampering, this room is a private and intimate sanctuary for most and is certainly worth lavishing extra thought and investment on.

___ Post and beam structure is apparent.
___ Dry wall finish
___ Raised ceiling to match living areas beyond
___ Lowered ceiling to create more intimacy

___ Shower stall
___ Tub/shower combination
___ Bumpout tub
___ Corner tub
___ Whirlpool tub
___ Bidet
___ One sink only
___ His and hers sinks
___ Private toilet area
___ Vanity

Flooring
___ Wide plank (pine)
___ Hardwood
___ Tile
___ Other

Outside window: __ Yes __ No
___ Double-hung windows
___ Casement windows
___ Awning windows
___ Gliding windows
___ Fixed or picture window
___ Specialty window

©Yankee Barn Homes Photo by Rich Frutchey

In an interesting twist, a "half wall" behind the vanity leaves the bathroom open to the cathedral ceiling in the center of the home. For two people who love each other, being able to talk from a bedroom balcony to bathing spot is a welcome invasion of privacy. Two doors beyond lead to the bedroom and a private toilet.

©Suki Coughlin/ Paula McFarland Stylist

Three square windows form a triptych of light.

©Suki Coughlin/ Paula McFarland Stylist

Red white and blue within a beadboard framework add a nautical aura.

©Suki Coughlin/ Paula McFarland Stylist

Bare bulbs around a mirror provide a theatrical effect in this otherwise humble vanity area.

A corner whirlpool bath is big enough for two. Blue and white tones mingle for nautical effect, and create an atmosphere where one can drift out to sea while soaking.

A corner tub is a space saver, leaving a big chunk of central floor that adds to the impression of spaciousness.

One bare beam serves as reminder that the soaring ceiling beyond is timber supported. A tub can be tucked under eaves, where it protects tall people from walking into the roof.

A marble-topped table was converted to a sink stand, adding to the country feeling that fits naturally into timber-supported environments.

Two outside windows grace this tub area,
and are easily closed off for privacy.

Variety and texture are created in the use of wood stains,
tile, and paint in this warm and inviting area of the bath.

A bath suite includes a vanity area and
oval whirlpool tub, turning the master
bath into a true spa. The luxury is
highlighted by an artful chandelier and
matching sconces.

Skylights and casement windows turn a soaking spot into a virtual swimming hole for dreamers. A light finish on the wood acts as neutral tone to the rose walls and cream colored porcelain and ceiling.

©Suki Coughlin/ Paula McFarland Stylist

Photo by Lisanti Photography

©Suki Coughlin/ Paula McFarland Stylist

Yellow works with white for a daisy bright bathroom. Skylights introduce light into the narrow, yet towering space.

Rich, dark tones were used to add allure to this room, from the dark stain on the beams, to the redwood stain on the tub surround and the blue, floral wallpaper. Lace curtains frame the view without interrupting it.

His and hers sinks lend themselves
to peace and harmony, and a
speedier exit in the morning.

©Suki Coughlin/ Paula McFarland Stylist

©Yankee Barn Homes Photo by Paul Jeremias

Above: One of the oldest decorator tips, a cutout
adds space to a room. Right: Timber framing and a
soaring celing define this room as a bath "suite." An
incredible view is framed beyond the tub, adding all
the wall art this room could ever require.

©2003 F&E Schmidt

©Suki Coughlin/ Paula McFarland Stylist

A tub tucks neatly under the eaves. Glass walls around a shower
stall promote a sense of spaciousness. Right: Color on walls and
cabinetry make a unique and enticing statement.

©Suki Coughlin/ Paula McFarland Stylist

Additional Bedrooms

Regardless of the size of the house, three bedrooms are typical with an occasional two or four bedroom home. A small bedroom might be nine feet by ten feet. A medium size bedroom might be twelve feet by twelve feet. A larger bedroom might be thirteen feet by fifteen feet. Today's bedroom may become tomorrow's study or library.

©Suki Coughlin/ Paula McFarland Stylist

An additional bedroom may rarely be used, but it is an excellent place to put favorite antiques or other beloved items on display. The contrast of dark beams and white wall board is stunning.

Grandchildren are welcomed in a room ever-ready for their visits.

This room occassionally serves as a granddaughter's home away from home, but is often occupied by grandmom and a good book.

Decorative beams have been installed in this bedroom, in keeping with the post and beam character of the home.

A lofty hideaway is a great spot for display.

French doors call in a popular guest room/retreat.

A small corner of the loft has been set aside for daydreaming, with a little view to the outside, and some favorite pieces of folk art for inspiration. Structural beams double as display shelves.

Kids don't have to be told twice to go to bed in this house. A loft lures them up to a fantasy hideaway. Lots of natural light and looking glass make them feel as though they're perched in the treetops.

A second-floor retreat includes enormous picture windows.

Woodwork is the focus of a room lovingly adorned with antique furnishings and linens. The upper-floor retreat is a sophisticated stopover for family and friends.

Timbers define spaces warmed by wood paneling and blue tile and paint. Artful linens pick up the color and stripe themes.

Additional Rooms

You're just starting out: plan your dream home. You may have to cut corners later. You may want to plan for future additions. In any case, when working together to build a home, work toward your dream!

__ *Baths/Powder Rooms*
How many full baths? __
How many half baths? __

__ *Laundry*
Laundry areas can be located on the first floor, second floor, or basement.

Outside window: __ Yes __ No
- __ Walk-in
- __ Closet
- __ Combined with mudroom area
- __ In a bath or lavatory space

__ *Mudroom*
For families with children or people who love to garden, the mudroom is a fine way to keep the great outdoors where it belongs. Mudrooms are often close to the garage and open into the kitchen area. This helps in transport of groceries to pantry and refrigerator. It's a fine place to put shoe and coat racks, tucked out of sight.
- __ Between garage and house
- __ Outside passageway between kitchen and yard
- __ Doubles as laundry
- __ Doubles as kid's craft room

__ *Garage*
Garages are typically twenty-four feet by twenty-four feet, which allow for two cars and additional storage. Garages can be expanded to have additional second floor space by adding knee walls to the second floor level or by adding dormers. For economy, or because of a difficult site, you may choose to place your garage under the main home.
- __ How many cars do you want to store in your garage?
- __ Include additional work or storage space?
- __ Part of the house
- __ Detached

__ *Garage Attic*

__ *Screened Porch*

__ *Home Theater*

__ *Gameroom*

__ *Spa/Exercise Room*

__ *In-law Suite*

__ *Barn for Animals*

Additional bathrooms are a great selling point in homes. Remember: the first thing listed in "house for-sale" ads is the number of bedrooms and baths. If you may ever need to sell the home, it should have the facilities to accommodate buyers.

Pool tables require a fair-sized room, with plenty of clearance. The luxury is worth the investment for a famiy that will actually use the space. A game of billiards is a wonderful opportunity to escape the television, to talk, and to play.

Lofts/Attics

One of the wonderful opportunities offered in building a timber frame home is an open loft area. Having installed gorgeous beams, why would anyone cover them up to create an attic? One would logically want to push storage areas to the darker, nether regions of the home. A loft is where ideas take flight. Following are some images that illustrate how others have utilized their elevated bonus spaces.

©2003 F&E Schmidt

A network of stairs and landings wind around the central stone chimney, offering an atmosphere of discovery among this home's rooms and open lofts.

©Keith Scott Morton

A family room/home office is tucked neatly under the eaves. The television alignment is set to entertain while dad burns the midnight oil on special projects.

©Yankee Barn Homes Photo by Paul Jeremias

©Suki Coughlin/ Paula McFarland Stylist

A roundtop window is the jewel set in symmetrical timber framing. This lofty office space has huge visual impact, and the ability to inspire. Right: A skylight and small casement windows light this attic hideaway.

A computer station and reading chair are perfect furnishings for a petite loft space. This is the homeowner's favorite hangout.

©Suki Coughlin/ Paula McFarland Stylist

Ground Works

You will return to the following pages again and again.

The first thing your designer will want to do is to establish what significant rooms you want on the ground floor. The rest of the house will be built upon the foundation of ground-floor rooms the homeowner requires.

The following checklist establishes which rooms you want on the first floor (1st), which on the second (2nd), which in the finished or walkout basement (B). On first thought, you'll probably imagine how convenient it would be to have everything on one level. But unless a rambling ranch is what you want, you're going to end up stacking rooms. Perhaps you've always envisioned all your bedrooms on the second floor, but if you're thinking of growing old in this house, you might want your master suite at ground level.

In addition to assigning rooms to their respective floors, you'll also want to give some thought to your space needs for each room. Like most people, you're probably at a loss to visualize the dimensions. It might help to go pace out rooms that you currently have. Obviously, when it comes to fitting everything within the exterior walls of your home, there will have to be adjustments made.

For starters, just check a line assigning a room to a floor. Later, as you work your way room-by-room through your dream home design, you can come back and pencil in rough dimensions for each room.

Remember, work in pencil so you can come back and fill in or change the details as you go.

How Big?

Usage options and total cost are implicit in the square feet planned for your home. To the extent that your budget permits, keep the square foot question open for a while. The ultimate cost of the house is also determined by your finishing selections.

The turn-key cost for a Yankee Barn in 2004 typically was $140-$180 per square foot, (count 25% of a garage, 25% of covered porches and 150% of floor space under vaulted ceilings as square feet). This cost estimate includes the foundation, but not the site work. Site work includes improvements such as the septic system, driveway, excavation, utilities, and landscaping.

Two thousand square feet is regarded as the minimum size for a three-bedroom, two-bath home. Yankee Barns tend to range from about two thousand square feet to six thousand plus square feet. The length of a Yankee Barn tends to be forty-five to sixty feet long. The width of the main structure is typically twenty-five feet, twenty-six feet, or thirty feet wide. The main structure's first floor is readily widened up to about eight feet by extending the roof line out to the side. The main structure's first or second floor can also be expanded with the use of dormers. Most Yankee Barns extend the living space with ells, wings, and connectors.

Starter List

Select the level (basement, first, or second floor) on which you envision the following rooms. If you don't need a room, simply leave that line unchecked.

B	1st	2nd	
____	____	____	Entry Foyer
____	____	____	Kitchen
____	____	____	Eat-in-Kitchen
____	____	____	Pantry
____	____	____	Breakfast Nook
____	____	____	Formal Dining Room
____	____	____	Great Room
____	____	____	Formal Living Room
____	____	____	Family Room
____	____	____	Home Office/Den
____	____	____	Master Bedroom
____	____	____	Master Bath
____	____	____	Bedroom
____	____	____	Bedroom
____	____	____	Bedroom
____	____	____	Bedroom
____	____	____	Full Bath
____	____	____	Full Bath
____	____	____	Powder Room
____	____	____	Laundry
____	____	____	Mudroom
____	____	____	Garage
____	____	____	Attic Over Garage
____	____	____	Attic Over House
____	____	____	Basement
____	____	____	Media Room/Home Theater
____	____	____	Game Room
____	____	____	Spa/Exercise Room
____	____	____	Sunroom
____	____	____	Deck off living/dining areas
____	____	____	Deck off master bedroom
____	____	____	In-law Suite
____	____	____	Barn for Animals
____	____	____	Estimated Total Square Feet

The Basic Floor Plan

A floor plan establishes the basic blueprint for a home. For the architect, it's the framework on which all the elements are hung. For the homeowner, it is a visual map to their new lifestyle. Following are a few sample floor plans to give you some idea of how your house might be laid out. After looking these over and getting an idea of how they work to convey information, you might try creating your own rough floor plan. Graph paper follows at the back of the book to enable you to rough in your own exterior walls, then pencil in where your rooms might fit. You might want to use tracing paper in order to create and recreate the basic outlines.

Plot Your Home

Photocopy these two pages and play. The graphics shown give average sizes, all on a 1/4-inch=one foot scale. If you have specific pieces of furniture you want to accommodate, measure them and make your own cutouts. Buy "furnishing" your rooms before you build, you will have a better sense of how you fit into your house. You may also save a lot of money by not having to rush out and buy new furniture because the old simply doesn't fit. On the following pages, sample floor plans and elevation drawings will help you visualize your dream home. Have fun!

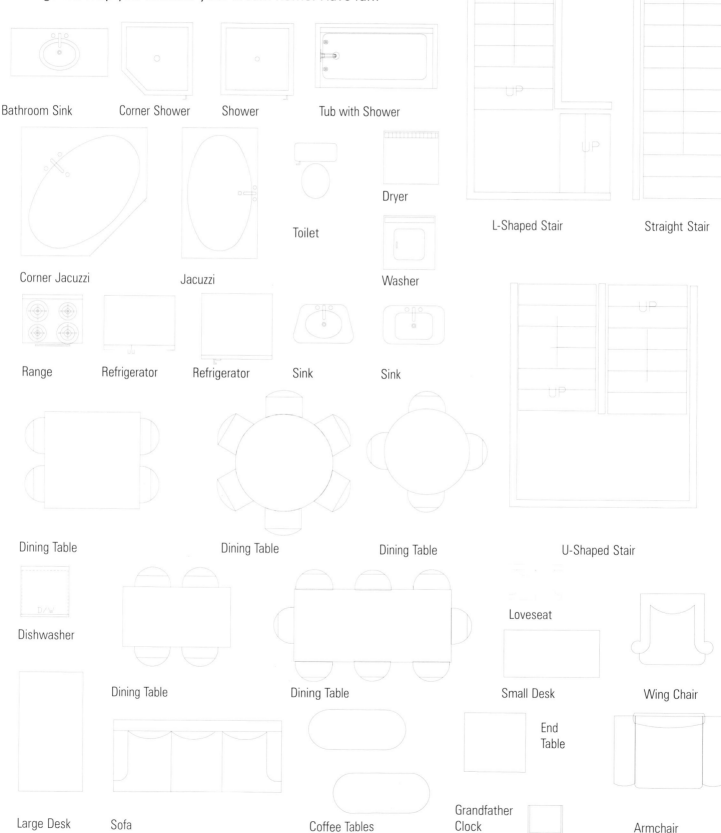

Bathroom Sink

Corner Shower

Shower

Tub with Shower

Corner Jacuzzi

Jacuzzi

Toilet

Dryer

Washer

L-Shaped Stair

Straight Stair

Range

Refrigerator

Refrigerator

Sink

Sink

Dining Table

Dining Table

Dining Table

U-Shaped Stair

Dishwasher

Dining Table

Dining Table

Loveseat

Small Desk

Wing Chair

End Table

Large Desk

Sofa

Coffee Tables

Grandfather Clock

Armchair

Bench

Six-shelf Bookcase

Double Bed

King Bed

Twin Bed

Queen Bed

Sample Floor Plans and Elevations

Foyer Side Elevation

Great Room Side Elevation

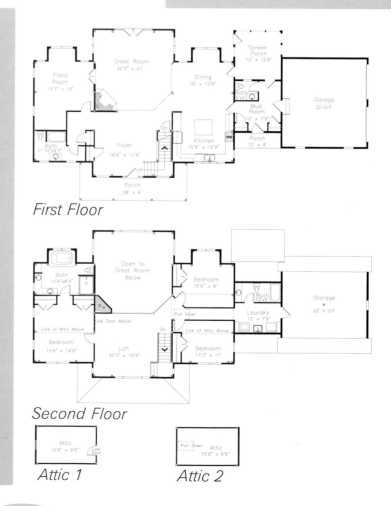

First Floor

Second Floor

Attic 1

Attic 2

Entry Side Elevation

Living Room End Elevation

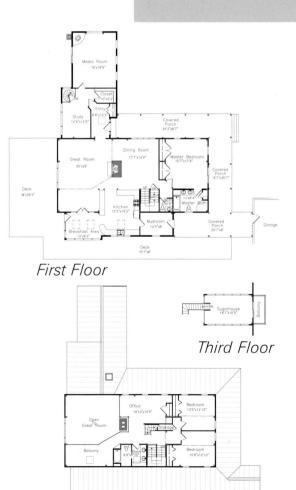

First Floor

Third Floor

Second Floor

Entry Side Elevation

Great Room Side Elevation

First Floor

Second Floor

Entry Side Elevation

Great Room Side Elevation

Bedroom End Elevation

First Floor

Master Bedroom
15'10"x17'1"

Great Room
20'x14'5"

Dining Room
16'x13'

Laundry
7'4"x7'5"

Master Bath
9'3"x9'8"

Closet
6'3"x9'8"

Wet Bar

Kitchen
16'x14'

Garage
27'3"x23'

Lav.

UP 14 Risers

7'4"x10'

Mudroom

Entry
11'x5'

Porch
8'x4'8"

Second Floor

Office
15'10"x12'4"

Open to Great
Room Below

Bedroom
16'x16'

Bedroom
15'10"x12'4"

Balcony
19'9"x12'5"

Bath
11'4"x5'3"

Great Room End Elevation

Porch Side Elevation

First Floor

Sewing Room
12'4"x12'11"

Office
12'5"x12'11"

Existing Structure

Dining Room
25'x14'2"

DN

Sunroom
19'x7'8"

Great Room
25'x15'1"

Wrap Around Porch

Second Floor

Guest Room
12'4"x12'11"

Bath
12'8"x9'3"

Existing Structure

Study
14'10"x13'10"

Open to
Great Room
Below

Balcony
7'10"x14'

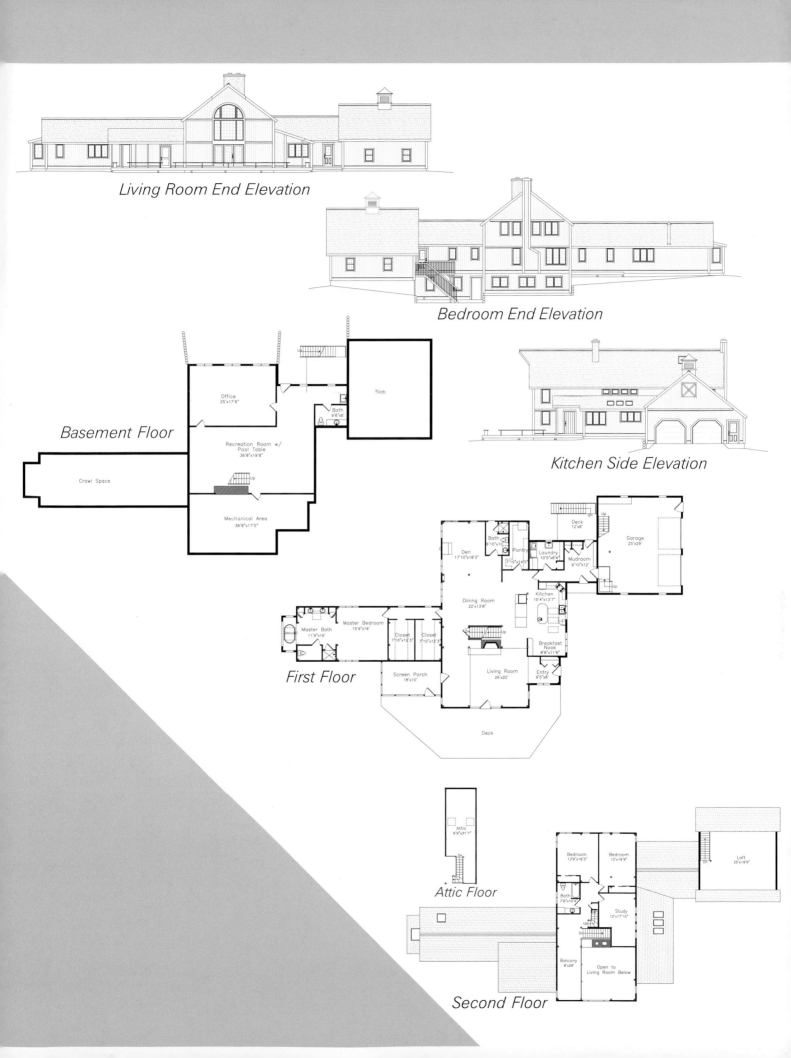

Living Room End Elevation

Bedroom End Elevation

Kitchen Side Elevation

Basement Floor

Office
25'x17'6"

Bath
9'6"x6'

Slab

Recreation Room w/
Pool Table
36'8"x19'8"

Up

Crawl Space

Mechanical Area
36'8"x17'5"

First Floor

Master Bath
11'9"x16'

Master Bedroom
15'9"x16'

Closet
7'10"x12'3"

Closet
7'10"x12'3"

Den
17'10"x18'3"

Bath
6'10"x10'

Pantry
7'10"x14'5"

Laundry
10'5"x8'4"

Deck
12'x8'

Dn   Up

Garage
25'x29'

Mudroom
9'10"x12'

Dining Room
22'x13'8"

Kitchen
15'4"x13'7"

Up

Breakfast
Nook
8'8"x11'6"

Living Room
26'x20'

Entry
9'5"x8'

Screen Porch
18'x10'

Deck

Attic Floor

Attic
9'9"x31'7"

Dn

Second Floor

Bedroom
13'9"x16'3"

Bedroom
12'x19'9"

Loft
25'x19'6"

Dn

Bath
7'6"x10'4"

Study
12'x17'10"

Up

Dn

Balcony
8'x29'

Open to
Living Room Below

Foyer Side Elevation

Living Room End Elevation

First Floor

Second Floor

Attic Floor

Entry Side Elevation

Great Room Side Elevation

Garage
23'x37'

Lav

Up

Pantry
7'9"

Kitchen
8'3" x 16'3"

Breakfast Nook
8'3" x 16'3"

Great Room
15'6" x 16'3"

Dining Room
15' x 16'9"

Up

Down

Master Bath
16'3" x 7'9"

Master Bedroom
16'9" x 17'

Walk-in Closet
7'6" x 13'

Entry
5'6" x 9'9"

First Floor

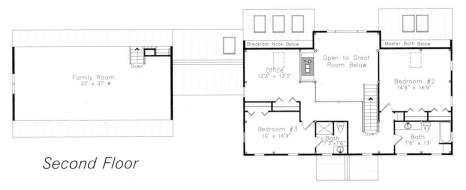

Family Room
23' x 37'

Down

Breakfast Nook Below

Office
12'3" x 13'3"

Open to Great
Room Below

Master Bath Below

Bedroom #2
14'9" x 16'9"

Bedroom #3
10' x 16'9"

Bath
7'3"x7'6"

Down

Bath
7'6" x 13'

Second Floor

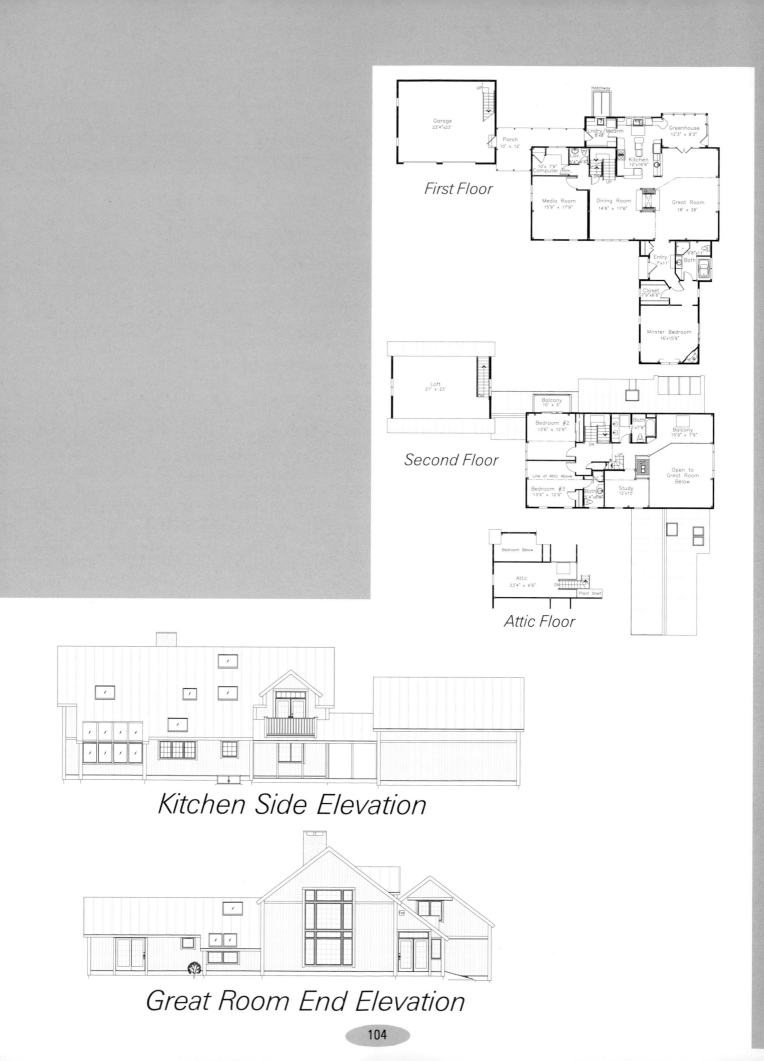

First Floor

Garage
23'4"x23'

Porch
10' x 12'

Lndry/Mudrm
8'x8'

Greenhouse
12'3" x 9'3"

Lav.
4'x4'6"

Kitchen
12'x16'9"

10'x 7'9"
Computer Rm.

Media Room
15'9" x 17'9"

Dining Room
14'6" x 17'6"

Great Room
18' x 26'

Entry
7'x11'

9'8"x11'
Bath

Closet
7'9"x6'6"

Master Bedroom
16'x15'9"

Hatchway

Second Floor

Loft
27' x 23'

Balcony
10' x 5'

Bedroom #2
13'6" x 12'9"

Bath
12'x7'9"

Balcony
15'9" x 7'9"

Line of Attic Above

Bedroom #3
13'6" x 12'9"

Bath
4'x8'

Study
12'x10'

Open to
Great Room
Below

Attic Floor

Bedroom Below

Attic
23'4" x 9'6"

Plant Shelf

Kitchen Side Elevation

Great Room End Elevation

Great Room Side Elevation

Kitchen End Elevation

First Floor

Entrance
18'9" x 7'6"

Covered Porch
43'4" x 8'6"

Guest Bedroom
12'x16'3"

Bath

Library/Media Room
16'6"x 13'

Lav.

Mudroom
8'8"x 11'8"

Laundry
8'x10'

Deck

DN

UP

Sunroom
15'x 12'6"

Great Room
24'x24'

Dining Room
17'x20'

Pantry

Kitchen
17'3" x 12'9"

Deck

Deck

Second Floor

Bedroom
14'3" x 10'

UP

DN

Office
8'6"x 9'6"

Closet
11'9"x 12'3"

Master Bedroom
18'9"x 17'6"

Bath
9'10" x 6'3"

Office
15'x 13'3"

Balcony
26' x 10'

Line of Attic Above

Master Bath
25' x 12'3"

Open to
Great Room
Below

Cupola Above

Attic
45'x 10'4"

Attic
10'x 10'4"

shelf @ Attic height

DN

Attic Floor

Entry Side Elevation

Bedroom End Elevation

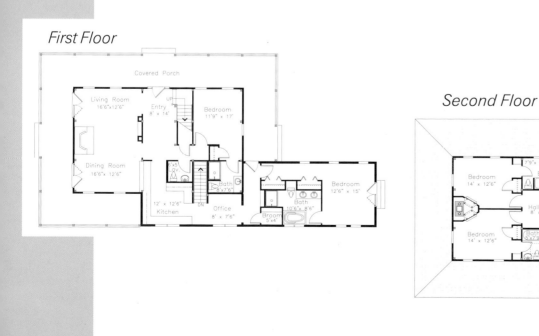

First Floor

Covered Porch

Living Room
16'6"x12'6"

Entry
8' x 14'

UP

Bedroom
11'9" x 17'

Dining Room
16'6" x 12'6"

Bath
8'x7'6"

12' x 12'6"
Kitchen

DN

Office
8' x 7'6"

Broom
5'x4'

Bath
10'6"x 8'6"

Bath

Bedroom
12'6" x 15'

Second Floor

Bedroom
14' x 12'6"

7'9"x 7'6"
Bath

Bedroom
11'9" x 9'9"

Hallway
8' x 9

DN

Bedroom
14' x 12'6"

Bath
5"x7'9"

Bath
5"x7'9"

Bedroom
11'9"x 9'9"

Dining Room Side Elevation

Kitchen End Elevation

First Floor

Bath
6'x7'6"

Entry
9'6"x7'6"

UP

Kitchen
13' x 9'

Living Room
18' x 22'

Dining Area
13' x 7'6"

Second Floor

Bath
9'x8'

DN

Balcony
20' x 12'

Bedroom
10' x 16'

Master Bedroom
20' x 12'

Sunroom Side Elevation

Entry Side Elevation

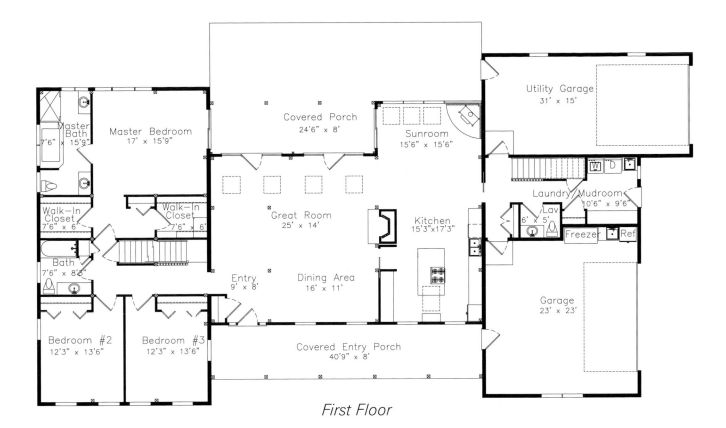

First Floor

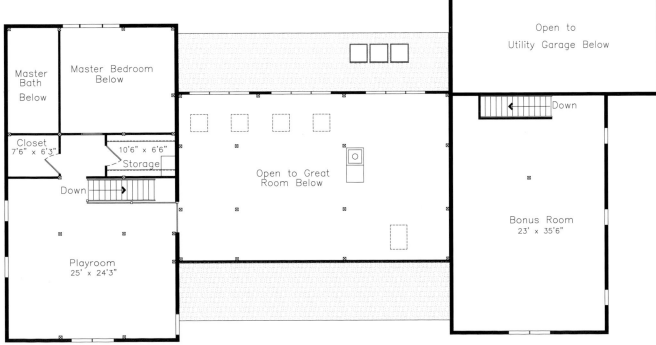

Second Floor

Entry Side Elevation

*Great Room
End Elevation*

First Floor

Covered Porch
16' x 5'

Kitchen
13'6" x 9'9"

Bath
6 x 6

Laundry/
Utility
11'9" x 9'6"

W D

Deck
10' x 32'

Great Room
16' x 26'

Up

Sauna
9'6" x 6'9"

Exercise Room
15'9" x 13'3"

Sitting Area
9' x 9'3"

Entry
6'6"x9'6"

Second Floor

Covered Porch Below

Bedroom #3
10' x 10'

Bath
6'3"x9'6"

Master
Bath
8'9"x9'6"

Walk-
In
Closet
6'6"x9'6"

Open to
Great Room
Below

Closet

Dn

Up

Closet

Master Bedroom
15'9" x 20'3"

Bedroom #2
15'9" x 10'

Bedroom #3
Below

Bath
Below

Master Bath
Below

Walk-In
Closet
Below

Open to
Great Room
Below

Dn

Attic
21'6" x 10'3"

Bedroom #2
Below

Master Bedroom
Below

Third Floor

Kitchen Side Elevation

Great Room End Elevation

First Floor

Second Floor

Porch End Elevation

Living Room Side Elevation

First Floor

Screened Porch
8'x 18'

Trash Storage

Kitchen 13'3"x8'3"

Trap Door

Pull Down Stairs

Bath
12'x 11'9"

Entry
9'10"x4'10"

Living Room
19'6" x 10'9"

Bedroom
12'x 12'

Screened Porch
8'x 50'

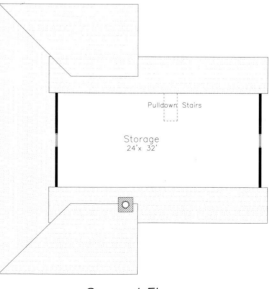

Pulldown Stairs

Storage
24'x 32'

Second Floor